Llewellyn's

2022
Witches'
Companion

A Guide to Contemporary Living

Llewellyn Publications is a registered trademark of Llewellyn Worldwide Ltd.

Art Director: Lynne Menturweck
Cover art © Tim Foley
Cover designer: Lynne Menturweck

Interior illustrations:
Tim Foley: 9, 23, 56, 63, 94, 129, 138, 174, 199, 212, 243
Bri Hermanson: 37, 76, 118, 153, 191, 250
Rik Olson: 31, 65, 104, 147, 181, 221
M. Kathryn Thompson: 11, 50, 86, 123, 162, 203, 232

ISBN 978-0-7387-6054-4

Llewellyn Worldwide Ltd. does not participate in, endorse, or have any authority or responsibility concerning private business transactions between our authors and the public.

Any internet references contained in this work are current at publication time, but the publisher cannot guarantee that a specific location will continue to be maintained. Please refer to the publisher's website for links to authors' websites and other sources.

You can order Llewellyn annuals and books from *New Worlds*, Llewellyn's magazine catalog. To request a free copy of the catalog, call toll-free 1-877-NEW-WRLD or visit our website at www.llewellyn.com.

Llewellyn Publications
A Division of Llewellyn Worldwide Ltd.
2143 Wooddale Drive
Woodbury, MN 55125-2989
www.llewellyn.com

Printed in the United States of America

Contents

Magical Self-Care

Nurture Your Body, Mind & Spirit

Witchy Living

Day-by-Day Witchcraft

Witchcraft Essentials

Practices, Rituals & Spells

The Lunar Calendar

September 2021 to December 2022

Community Forum

PROVOCATIVE OPINIONS ON
CONTEMPORARY TOPICS

Witchcraft & Social Media: Should You Share Your Personal Practice?

Kate Freuler

Have you ever shared pictures or videos of your personal spells on social media? If so, do you feel it had an effect on the outcome of the working? Do you suspect that some of the perfect altar photos in your feed are staged just to get views and likes?

These are questions many of us are asking ourselves as we traverse a world in which the relationship between a person's real life and their online persona has become complicated. Balancing sacred spirituality with the ever-changing, competitive world of social media can be a daunting task, and when the two worlds collide, things can get a little weird.

Back when I began learning about witchcraft, my biggest challenge was finding informative books. This task sounds ridiculously simple compared to the present. Nowadays there are young witches attempting to curse the moon, experienced witches behaving badly in the comments section, cancel culture, the witch aesthetic, influencer witches, and the monetization of spiritual services. There are innumerable online magick courses promising adept supreme status for a fee, and video tutorials showing how to hex your enemies. There's more information than one person can possibly sift through, never mind finding an informative book. (And after you do finally find a book you like, you're apt to discover a bunch of videos of witches explaining why it's the wrong one.)

For those of us who've made it past this onslaught of conflicting information and developed a daily practice, our spirituality is usually inextricably entwined with our daily life. Therefore, to be ourselves online can mean exposing our deeply held beliefs in a way that can be either wonderful or terrible, depending on how others react to it. This makes using social media a little different for magickal people. After all, there's a big difference between posting a cute picture of your cat versus an intimate, emotionally charged love spell.

Everybody's different. Some practitioners choose to keep their work completely private and never snap a single photo. Other witches are comfortable occasionally sharing their altar setup. Some

> **Our spirituality is usually inextricably entwined with our daily life. Therefore, to be ourselves online can mean exposing our deeply held beliefs in a way that can be either wonderful or terrible, depending on how others react to it.**

witches film and broadcast every single working they do. There are even influencer witches who have completely integrated magick and media into a single formidable personality.

Despite the fact that spells and rituals are a normal, everyday part of our lives, they're still considered strange by many outsiders, so the decision to expose them to public scrutiny needs to be considered carefully. The level of social media that people allow in their craft ranges across a broad spectrum, and so do the opinions about it. There is no way to tell another person the correct approach, because what works for one witch doesn't necessarily work for another.

The Power of Thought

Sharing a photo of your beautiful crystal grid or a well-made spell candle can be empowering, especially when people engage through likes and positive comments. However, something that has crossed my mind, and probably yours, is to wonder if overtly broadcasting a magickal working to anyone and everyone could possibly lessen its authenticity or even weaken its power—not to mention the logistical problem of having to halt mid-spell, break your focus, and take a bunch of pictures.

Thoughts and feelings are energy. Energy impacts everything it touches. A person's thoughts could possibly, then, impact your working, even if that person is on the other side of the world. If someone, somewhere, looks at your spell picture and feels a negative emotion toward you and it, will this interfere with your results? Every person who scrolls through your feed will see your spell and experience an emotion, sometimes good, sometimes bad. The problem is that you can't control which way it goes, and this leaves you vulnerable in a way.

For this reason, I'm careful about what I post and I share spells only long after they are completed. I'm of the opinion that thoughts sent toward me and my workings, even if only through a picture, can interfere with them. Not everyone agrees with this opinion, and that's okay.

Even if you don't believe that remote thoughts will affect your magick, there's always a chance that comments from strangers, especially negative remarks, will put a dent in your confidence. This can make you doubt yourself, which will affect the manifestation of your working.

Collective Belief

Some people choose to share every spell and ritual they partake in across all forms of social media. They feel that the more people that see the image, the more power it will gain. This is an interesting take and can be useful for groups who want to create large-scale change through magick that reaches many people. It can also be applied to empowering symbols and sigils.

The most powerful symbols are the ones that impact people immediately upon sight by invoking emotion. Popular symbols that have been around for a long time, such as a crucifix, the star of Baphomet, a pentacle, or even a skull and crossbones, have collected energy and power simply by being seen and understood for a long time. The meaning of the symbol and the emotion it triggers are imprinted on our minds. Imagine, then, what a sigil could do when passed from witch to witch, each person empowering it with the same meaning. As it's viewed and shared repeatedly all over the world, it accumulates energetic clout, gaining power with every repost. Think about all the things we could do with that power!

In recent years, magickal practitioners have used social media to organize worldwide rituals where everyone agrees to perform a spell simultaneously at a specified time from wherever they happen to live. The idea is that when so many people communally partake in raising energy, it will have a huge impact on a global scale. This kind of large group working would have been impossible to arrange twenty-five years ago, and it's interesting to follow along and see the results. It's definitely one of the perks of social media for witches.

Some Positive Points

It's tempting to approach social media with a dubious attitude, because it can be toxic and damaging. It encourages unrealistic beauty standards, triggers unhealthy comparisons between ourselves and others, and is often fake. But it also has a positive side.

For many witches, their whole community is online. They simply don't have anyone nearby who shares their interests, so social media brings an important sense of connection. It also provides many teachers and mentors. You can learn so many things about different traditions just by following along with various social media accounts. Many witches share facts, experiences, and instructions, making learning quicker than ever (and free). If witches never went public with their practice, then none of this knowledge would be readily available.

Having online friends has become the new normal. You might find that you really click with certain people, and the next thing you know, you have a whole witchy support system. Your online witch friends will get it when you say things like, "I saw a cat shape in a candle flame this morning—something big is coming my way!" or "I set off all the smoke alarms while cleansing my house again." That kind of friendship is priceless.

How Much Is Too Much?

If you choose to share your workings on social media, you may become well known and gain a lot of followers. This can be exciting and empowering. After all, if likes and hearts didn't give us a boost of serotonin, none of us would be doing it. But thanks to the algorithms at play, it also creates pressure to produce content in order to build and maintain your following. When you have lots of followers or are trying to get more, you're expected to deliver a constant stream of interesting, aesthetically pleasing, informative material that others can relate to. Over time, the demand to create for other people's consumption rather than your own spiritual reasons may take away from the authenticity of your content and lead you to burn out. Worse, it might cause you to compromise your own beliefs in order to please others and follow trending opinions you don't actually resonate with. If you find yourself scrambling to stage witchy-looking setups, creating altars and spell pics with the thought of followers in mind instead of your own practice, it might be time to step away from it. However, if you love staging photos and it's making your life better, then by all means keep going!

Being an influencer is one of the most sought-after occupations today. It sounds great in theory. Imagine having so many people who adore you complimenting you constantly and sending you gifts and free products, and earning tons of money just by living your life and taking selfies.

If you become really well known, sometimes people forget that you're an actual person with feelings and boundaries. Influencer witches and mystical people often end up doing a lot of emotional work on behalf of their followers.

However, there's a downside to all of that attention. If you become really well known, sometimes people forget that you're an actual person with feelings and boundaries. Influencer witches and mystical people often end up doing a lot of emotional work on behalf of their followers, feeling obligated to respond to every question, message, like, and comment. When people look up to you as wise, they will come to you with their problems, seeking counseling and advice. Some will even think they're entitled to your time and energy. You might find yourself spending hours answering messages and getting nothing in return but exhaustion. This is exactly why some well-known witches charge a fee for their time, advice, and counsel in the form of readings or seer services.

Protect Yourself

Here are some ideas for protecting your online life from interference:

- Consider sharing really personal workings only with a list of friends you know you can trust. These are people who will send positive, supportive energy your way. Many apps allow you to create groups with whom you can directly share your posts, so only chosen people can view them.

- If you're worried that your spell will be harmed by the thoughts of others, don't share it until after it has manifested or is totally complete. You can post about it after the fact, if you want, knowing it's already done and safe from interference.

- If you find you're being inundated with messages requesting your help and insight, consider turning off your inbox for a while. Make an announcement and then stick to your allotted time to be unavailable. This is setting a healthy boundary for your own self-care, and those who truly value you will respect it.

- Create a protective symbol and discreetly place it on the device you most commonly use for social media. Draw the symbol on a bit of paper and conceal it inside your phone case where no one can see it.

- Avoid stopping mid-spell to snap a photo. This interrupts the entire working. If you must record it, set your phone on a tripod nearby and let it record. After the spell has manifested, you can share the video or a still photo from it.

- Be mindful of what you forward from other people's feeds. It can be tempting to jump in on popular issues and share memes and other content without actually researching the source or background. Do a quick fact-check before jumping on any bandwagons, because sometimes these trends do more harm than good.

- Avoid contacting big-name witches unless it's for something really important. Their inbox is guaranteed to be full, and they might not see your message. When they don't respond, it can feel like a slap in the face, leading to a sense of disconnection from community. Feeling unseen sucks, so don't set yourself up for it. Focus on learning and growing your own practice.

- Be careful whom you listen to. No matter how cool and popular someone seems on social media, everyone is fallible and makes mistakes. No single individual is all-knowing or has all the "right" answers. Before putting all of your energy into backing them, think about researching topics on your own as well, so you can build your own beliefs.

- The oldest advice still stands: Don't feed the trolls!

Kate Freuler *lives in Ontario, Canada, and is the author of* Of Blood and Bones: Working with Shadow Magick & the Dark Moon. *She owns and operates White Moon Witchcraft (www.whitemoonwitchcraft.com), an online witchcraft boutique. When she isn't crafting spells and amulets for clients or herself, she loves to write, paint, read, draw, and create.*

Illustrator: M. Kathryn Thompson

Do You Worship the Devil?
And Other Questions You
Might Be Asked

James Kambos

It was Christmas 1989. My mom, who was so cool, knowing that I was interested in the occult and magic, ordered me a book about Witchcraft from Llewellyn. I, needless to say, thought it was awesome. Later that day when family dropped by, some of them noticed the book.

Gasp! The barrage of questions began:

Do you worship the Devil?

Do you cast spells?

Do you believe in Heaven and Hell?

Do you believe in God?

The questions went on and on.

Some people asked questions because they were fearful and didn't understand. Other folks asked me questions because they, too, were interested in following a magical path but didn't know where to start. Some people just wanted to be nosy.

That's when I knew I'd better be prepared to answer a lot of questions if I was going to choose to live a magical life.

As time went on, I realized that some people had some genuinely thoughtful questions about magic and the Craft. Some people asked questions because they were fearful and didn't understand. Other folks asked me questions because they, too, were interested in following a magical path but didn't know where to start. Some people just wanted to be nosy. Finally, some idiots asked questions just so they could be a jerk.

If you're reading this, chances are you've had similar experiences. Some of the questions you'll be asked are truly thought-provoking, some are amusing, and some are just plain nuts.

To help you respond to some of the questions you may encounter or to deal with some of the comments you'll hear, I'm going to share some of my thoughts. These are a few tips on how you can handle some of the more popular topics you might come up against.

I've found, over time, that most of the questions and comments I've dealt with usually fall into one of these three categories:

• Spirituality

• Magic

• How to become a Witch

Some of these may overlap, but I'll do my best to cover some of the major themes in each category and how I've answered the more popular questions. I'll start with spirituality.

Spirituality

This topic is loaded with questions. I can only answer a few. I'll start with the one I hear the most.

DO YOU WORSHIP THE DEVIL?

If asked this, say *no*! Then explain to the individual that with all the horror films and books about the topic, you understand how they've been misinformed. I always explain that Witches do believe in a god of nature and the hunt called the *Horned God*, but this has no connection to the Devil. Also, when asked this, explain that the Devil is actually a Christian concept. This should assure your listener that there is no Devil worship in the Craft.

DO YOU BELIEVE IN GOD?

First explain that there are some Witches who are atheists. Then tell your listener such people are still considered valid Witches. But explain that most Witches do believe in a divine power. If you're unsure how to begin talking about the God/Goddess, I always start by saying that Witches believe in a balance of male/female forces in nature. Then it should be easier for you to talk about the belief in a dual divine power, which is the concept of the God and Goddess. If you feel the person you're speaking to is very new to the Craft, you may wait until later before you begin talking about specific deities.

WHAT ABOUT HEAVEN AND HELL?

When asked this question, if I were you, I would again explain that the concept of Heaven and Hell is of Christian origin. However, continue by saying that Witches do believe in good and evil. Many

Witches also believe in angelic and demonic forces. This is also a good time to point out to non-magical folks what many Witches believe happens to the soul after the death of the physical body. Depending on what you believe, you might say you believe the soul travels to the Other Side, or Summerland, instead of Heaven or Hell. At this point, I usually say that after rest and renewal, the soul is reincarnated. I've found that these days, more people of different faiths are a little more accepting of the reincarnation idea than in the past. But you must say what you feel comfortable with depending on the situation.

Do You Pray?

A friend once said to me, "You don't pray, do you?" Meaning that Witches don't pray. I suggest that if you are faced with this question, say something like, "Yes, but maybe not in the same way you do."

Explain that Witches usually say an affirmation, not a standard prayer. If you need to define it, just say that a prayer asks for help, but an affirmation is a statement that says you will get what you're asking for. Stress that we use affirmations to bring about positive results only.

Now let's take a look at some of the questions or comments you may hear about magic.

Magic

This is the category that may interest non-magical folks or newbies the most. It's also the category that can get them into trouble the most. If they start to dabble in the dark magical arts, they might not realize what they could be in for. That's why you have to answer questions or comments about magic carefully, starting with...

I Want to Be a Witch So I Can Cast Spells

When you hear this, a red flag should go up. First and foremost, you have a responsibility to tell someone who says this that there's more

to being a Witch than casting spells. Then explain that the Craft is a whole lifestyle that involves respect for nature and others. Magic is a small part of being a Witch. Next, guide them to authors you trust on the subject of spellcraft. Offer them guidance if they want it. Remember, you don't need to be a Witch to practice positive magic. Remind them that there are many Christians, for example, who practice powerful folk magic.

Will You Cast a Spell for Me?

Yikes! When you hear this question, beware. The reason I say this is because first, when someone wants you to cast a spell, it's usually because they're seeking some kind of revenge—against the nosy neighbor, the creepy boss, and let's not forget that dirty, rotten ex-lover. These, I've found, are some of the favorite targets. Second, if you do cast a spell for someone else and it doesn't work, they'll blame you! So, in a case like this, I gently explain that if they cast the spell themselves, it will be more powerful. If you want, you can offer to coach them on how to cast a positive protection spell.

I rarely cast spells for other people. An exception would be if it's someone I know really well and they ask for my help because they're going through a serious illness. In a case like this, if they feel that a spell would supplement proper medical treatment, then I'd be glad to help. Generally, my advice to you when someone wants you to do spellwork for them is to gently turn them down.

Discussions about magic frequently lead to the last category I'd like to talk about.

How to Become a Witch

How you respond to this life-changing step that someone is about to take depends on your experiences. This is how I've handled it when someone asks...

How Do I Become a Witch?

When someone asks you this, they're giving you their trust. I feel moved and humbled, because chances are this person may feel they have no one else to talk to. First, let them know there is no one right way to "become" a Witch. In fact, if they're asking this question, then they probably have somehow known all along that they've had these feelings. Next, direct them to read all they can not just about the Craft but also about other spiritual paths, in order to broaden their horizons and be informed. During this transition period, you may also encourage them to meditate, and you may recommend that they network with Pagan and magical groups, where they can ask a lot of questions.

Do I Have to Join a Coven?

When you hear this question, I hope you say *no*. Just let a new member of the Craft know they have options. You may point out the advantages of being in a coven or being a solitary. In a coven, for example, you share the work. As a solitary, you do what you want, when you want. I would also let those new to the Craft understand that they don't need to be initiated. If someone tells them otherwise, they should ask, "Who initiated the first Witch?" Point out to them that you can light a candle, pour a glass of wine, and toast the Old Gods, and you're just as much a Witch as anyone else.

These are just some of the questions or comments you may feel the need to address. Remember, when you respond in a thoughtful, calm manner, you become a positive representation of the Witch community.

James Kambos *is a solitary who writes and paints from his home in Appalachian Ohio. He has written numerous articles and essays about magic and herbalism. He holds a degree in history and geography from Ohio University.*

Illustrator: Tim Foley

Dealing with Doubt

Melanie Marquis

It's hard to keep having faith when it seems all prayers go unanswered, sincere efforts fail to bring desired results, and all spells seem to falter right on the brink of success. We all have doubts. We might doubt our chances for success. We might doubt the intentions or abilities of those around us. We might doubt our beliefs. We might doubt that anything will ever get better. Individually and collectively, we all experience troubling times that often lead to doubt. While some people may take comfort from the adage "Everything happens for a reason" or misuse the Christian mindset of "let go and let God" to justify giving up or detaching from personal responsibility, others find themselves descending into the shark-infested waters of doubt with no swimming skills, no boat, and no land in sight.

So how do we get past doubt without relying on blind faith or positive affirmations through which logical reasoning punches countless holes? The fact is there are only three possible responses to doubt. Whether we ignore the doubt or acknowledge it, we can either stop what we're doing, continue what we're doing, or change what we're doing.

Doubt does have a purpose. A tinge of doubt is often hard to distinguish from a twinge of intuition—both give us a physical sensation that lets us know an idea or a situation just isn't sitting right in our mind or our heart. Doubt allows us to analyze situations and ideas so we can adjust our approaches and strategies and more freely abandon those things that are no longer working for us or are likely to lead to disaster. Here are some strategies for making the most of doubt, and moving past it when appropriate.

Objective Analysis

The first strategy for dealing with doubt is to evaluate it. What is the nature of the doubt and where does it come from? Not all doubt is created equal! Some doubts are logical, while others stem from outdated insecurities and unfounded fears. Ask yourself objectively if your doubts are warranted, and if they're not, ask yourself where the sense of doubt most likely originated.

For example, I doubt that I could safely pilot an airplane. This doubt is warranted, justified, and totally logical, seeing as I've never taken pilot lessons and know virtually nothing about flying an airplane. No amount of confidence or positive affirmations will make me capable of safely operating an airplane. To move past the doubt of my flying abilities, I would need to train to become a pilot.

To take another example, I doubted at one point in my life that I could ever become a professional writer. I had good writing skills and a willingness to hone my craft, research the profession, and seek out opportunities for writing. I recognized that any doubt I had in regard to writing came from a place of personal insecurity and was not actually logical in light of my abilities and willingness to expend effort and patience until I reached my goal.

Since this doubt came from a place of insecurity, I had to look objectively at the reasons for that insecurity. Did I honestly believe that I was capable of writing? Yes, I did. Did I honestly believe that I had ideas to share that could benefit others? Yes, I did. Did I honestly believe that I should present myself as some sort of authority? No, I didn't—and I still don't, in fact! I believe I have a lot of knowledge and a lot of creative ideas that can help people see things in new ways, and I believe I understand very well the topics I write about. But I don't like to think of myself as an authority, putting myself above my readers. I instead want to empower people to be their own authority.

Evaluating all of these different layers and aspects of the doubt helped me realize who I am, and who I am not, when it comes to writing. Without that sense of doubt, I might not have ever really honed in on my voice and message as a writer. With the doubt, I've developed a very clear view of what I wish to accomplish with my writing. Doubt can help us to define ourselves and refine our plans in ways that will bring us closer to success.

Doubt can also serve as a powerful warning. Sometimes doubts arise to let us know that what we're doing or what we have in mind to do is simply not in our best interest. If you evaluate your doubts and find them to be founded in reality, then the next step is to decide whether or not those doubts should stop you. Is the potential reward worth the risks? Do you have any other options of possible actions you could take? Could the consequences of proceeding despite your doubts potentially lead to a cost that is too high to pay? It's important to remember that we can change our minds in life. We can change our plans, too. Sometimes a feeling of doubt is a message from our inner self to stop what we're doing, step back, reevaluate, and change course. You don't have to keep hanging on to dreams that are unlikely to ever come true. We sometimes need to let go of old dreams in order to make room for new ones.

Sometimes doubt seems to arise as a test—not a test of faith, but rather a test of determination. At times the universe appears to have a way of throwing potholes along our path with an exceptionally cruel sense of timing. Just as we think we're finally about to reach the top of a big hill and are getting excited for smoother sailing ahead, a giant boulder comes rolling over the top of that hill to knock us right back to the bottom again. These unexpected challenges and calamities that stand in the way of our progress force us to reevaluate our commitment to those goals. Are we willing to climb this hill all over again, and possibly again and again, or have we lost interest? Is it time to find a new hill to climb, or are we still committed to our chosen course?

> **Sometimes doubt seems to arise as a test—not a test of faith, but rather a test of determination.... Is it time to find a new hill to climb, or are we still committed to our chosen course?**

Obstacles are going to arise in the course of virtually any action we can take in life, and such obstacles are likely to cause feelings of doubt. If you keep pursuing your goal, even when faced with doubts and hardships, you will most likely eventually make progress toward achieving that goal. On the other hand, if you abandon your goal when any doubts or challenges arise, you're not likely to ever get anywhere. With each old goal abandoned and each new goal that takes its place, new challenges and new doubts will inevitably arise. Once you find a goal that you are willing to pursue at the cost of having to deal with whatever doubts and challenges the universe presents to you, you'll know you're on the right track and you've found your true calling. Nothing, after all, is easy, so make sure you're putting your efforts into a race that you actually care to win.

Sleep on It

One way to gain insight into the nature of doubt is to literally sleep on it, and hopefully dream about it. Write down on a piece of paper an expression of your doubt, and put this under your pillow before you fall asleep, with the intention in mind that your dreams will include insights regarding the situation. When you wake up, write down everything you remember from your dreams. Look for any symbols or patterns that can provide information about your circumstances.

If you don't remember your dreams, that's okay; your subconscious may still have gained some insight. Read over your written description of your doubt again and see how you feel about it. Have your feelings changed? Are you feeling more swayed in one direction or another? If you're still undecided, you can try this exercise again over the course of several nights to see if your ideas become any clearer.

Divining Your Doubts

Another technique for evaluating doubt is to employ divination. I personally prefer tarot cards for this, as the cards cover the full gamut of the human experience. Consider your doubt, mix the cards into a loose pile, and select any that seem to call to you. If you like, you can draw each card while thinking of a more specific question, such as "What is

the origin of this doubt?" or "What will I miss out on if I let this doubt stop me?" or "What will help me address this doubt?" Use your intuition and your natural response to each card's imagery as the first line of interpretation, then look up the meanings of the cards in several guidebooks to find further insights.

Magickal Persuasion

Magickal techniques to deal with doubt take many different forms. If the doubt is stemming from an insecurity or a fear that you would like to overcome, you might use magick to help increase your confidence or courage. If the doubt is manifesting as a response to an intuited or obvious obstacle that is likely to pose a challenge, you might use magick to help guide and support you through a tough situation or even transform the situation altogether.

As humans, we are not all-powerful, but we are indeed all filled with great power. Sometimes the webs we weave are ripped asunder; sometimes the temples we build crumble and collapse. Not every seed sprouts, and not every patch of soil provides a firm foundation. That is how it is in nature, and so it is in our own lives as well. Not everything is going to work out in our favor.

Sometimes you will try your very best and have unwavering faith and 100 percent positive thinking and things still won't work out as you want them to. But as long as you are a living, conscious being, you can't let doubts caused by past experiences limit your perception of your options for the present and the future. So what if you have failed before? So what if you fail again? The path to success often includes some failure, both ongoing and along the way.

Stopping at failure, letting your doubts stop you from trying to live your best life, leaves very little room for greater success to come. On the other hand, if you vow to keep trying until you succeed in your goals—while giving yourself the space and permission to change those goals at any time as you see fit—you will be virtually guaranteed to experience success in some form or another. It's like the artist who is perpetually painting a masterpiece—if it's never finished, who's to say it isn't a masterpiece?

While there are undoubtedly fairly objective indicators of what constitutes success versus failure in particular professions, activities, and other human endeavors, success and failure live largely in the mind. When things aren't going your way and you experience doubt, try to remember that you don't have to dwell on it. It's a cliché to say so, but there really often is a silver lining to failure. In other words, you don't have to cry about burning the bread; you can instead rejoice in the unexpected making of croutons. In dealing with doubt, it's important to recognize the positives of the situation so that bubbles of doubt don't artificially expand beyond due measure.

> **When things aren't going your way and you experience doubt, try to remember that you don't have to dwell on it.... In dealing with doubt, it's important to recognize the positives of the situation so that bubbles of doubt don't artificially expand beyond due measure.**

It's a Big World After All

Another way to look at doubt is to recognize it for what it is: a facet of perspective. Our lives are generally centered around our own life experiences and the life experiences of those around us, and when things aren't going well in our personal sphere, it can be tempting to believe that the whole world has become a terrible place. Sometimes the cosmos does seem to experience an overall negative slump, or the earth seems to be traveling along a very rough groove.

More often, though, when we're experiencing hardships, there is still plenty of goodness elsewhere. The world is actually a pretty big place, and it's a fact that at every moment of every day, there is something terrible happening somewhere and also something wonderful happening somewhere else. When we're consumed with doubt, it can be helpful to gain some perspective on the situation by remembering that our own experiences are only one tiny aspect of the overall world we're living in. What seems insurmountable at the moment may very well become tomorrow's memory of a doubt disproved and an obstacle overcome.

Melanie Marquis *is the creator of the* Modern Spellcaster's Tarot *(illustrated by Scott Murphy) and the author of several books, including* A Witch's World of Magick; The Witch's Bag of Tricks; Carl Llewellyn Weschcke: Pioneer and Publisher of Body, Mind & Spirit; Witchy Mama *(with Emily A. Francis);* Beltane; Lughnasadh; *and* Llewellyn's Little Book of Moon Spells. *The founder of United Witches Global Coven and a local coordinator for the Pagan Pride Project, Melanie loves sharing magick with others and has presented workshops and rituals to audiences across the US. She lives in Denver, Colorado.*

Illustrator: Rik Olson

Physics, Math & Magic: Balancing Your Existential Equations

Rev. J. Variable x/ø

Huzzah! The human race has finally evolved. We live in a peaceful utopia. We've conquered hatred, bigotry, climate change, and poverty. War is only a memory. We are truly a global community, coexisting in love and light and...

Well, anyway. It's a nice idea, isn't it?

But why is it *still* only an idea? Consider how many people have been praying and casting spells together over the years to create a perfect world like this: hundreds of thousands of minds and souls focusing their individual and combined energies toward the same enlightened intent. We know that magic is valid, thoughts have power, and reality is what we make of it. So why is the world still a mess? For that matter, why can't I even get one tiny little win-the-lotto spell to work?

Trapped in a Consensual Reality

Reality *is* what we make of it. Unfortunately, it is also what everyone *else* makes of it, too. There are trillions upon trillions of sentient beings on this planet alone: humans, animals, plants, and anything else that might have a mind of its own. Each of those sentient beings perceives the world with its own set of ideas and expectations.

Imagine all those minds pushing and tugging at reality, trying to get it to conform to their own notions, preconceived or learned, of how things *should* be. Imagine, too, reality pushing and tugging back on all those minds, reinforcing only what *can* be.

Most of our notions about *should be* and *can be* have been drilled into us from so far back in our own lives and across generations that we don't even think to question them: the sky is blue, it's *always been* blue, and it's *going to be* blue tomorrow and the next day.

What if you decide you want the sky to be purple instead? One night you get yourself all worked up to the point where you really, truly believe that the sky is going to be purple tomorrow. You have the utmost confidence in your ability to influence reality. The next day you wake up, go outside, and…behold!

The stupid sky is still blue.

The problem isn't that you're not trying hard enough; the problem is that a billion other people are still expecting a blue sky. If you're honest with yourself, so are you. Wishful thinking doesn't stand a chance against opposing forces like that.

Our communal existence is the result of all these unique perceptions: a lowest-common-denominator world where what you want has little influence over a reality dictated by everyone's *expectations*.

Imagination and intent are key factors in magic, but it's going to take more than these to make a real difference. Forget mystery and miracles for the moment—we need a scientific approach.

Newton's Laws of Magic

"Newton was not the first of the age of reason. He was the last of the magicians." —John Maynard Keynes, 1942

Isaac Newton spent his life studying the forces and interactions of the world in which we live every day. His contribution to classical physics (that which governs the world we can actually see, as opposed to *quantum* physics*) was so groundbreaking that the field is often simply called Newtonian physics.

Physics deals with the qualities and interactions of three things: mass, force, and energy.

- **Mass** tells us how much matter, or "stuff," is in an object. (This is not the same as weight. Weight changes if gravity changes; mass does not.)

- **Force** describes interactions between masses or other forces. Force can take many forms, each with its own set of effects.

- **Energy** also has a lot of different forms and definitions. Essentially, it describes a force's potential to do work: to make a change in a system. A force's energy depends on its strength, its direction, and the inertia (resistance to change) of the object or system that we wish to change (or to prevent from changing).

---

* The links, credible and otherwise, between magic and quantum physics have been explored so much lately that I'm not even going to go into that here. However, many wishful thinkers have hitched a ride on quantum physics' coattails to "prove" their ideas. I urge quantum enthusiasts to read up on the strictly scientific side of it before accepting such claims.

Mass, force, and energy are the keystones of Newton's three laws of motion, which he published in 1687 in his book *Philosophiae Naturalis Principia Mathematica*. These concepts also work very well to describe the essential mechanics of magic and reality. *Mass* defines the perspectives and expectations that create a state of localized or global reality. *Force* is the power of your spells and thoughts. The more forceful your spells, the greater their *energy*, and the better your chances of affecting reality's mass.

The Clockwork Universe

Newton showed us that the universe is like a big clockwork machine. We can know anything about the past or future states of any given system if we know enough about its condition in the present. In other words, objects and forces will obey the rules of physics, so if we know all the variables in a system's current state, we can just do a little math to determine its state at any point in its timeline. Math doesn't care if we're going forward or backward.

Newton's First Law of Motion: Every body perseveres in its state of rest, or of uniform motion in a right line, unless it is compelled to change that state by forces impressed thereon.

This law is fairly simple. If an object (mass) is sitting still, it's going to continue to do so until some force makes it move.

If an object is moving, it will continue moving, in a straight line, at the same speed, until some force stops or changes it.

An object's resistance to a change in its state of motion (or non-motion) is called its *inertia*. The more inertia an object has, the more difficult it is to start it, stop it, speed it up, slow it down, or change its direction. The most important thing that affects an object's inertia is the amount of mass it has—the more mass, the more the object can resist a change.

The equation looks like this:

$F = ma$
The force (F) is equal to the mass (m) multiplied by the acceleration (a).

First Law of Magical Motion: Every individual or consensual perception of reality continues along the expected, predictable, most likely path unless it is compelled to change by forces impressed upon it.

Reality has inertia! Life tends to stay the same unless new forces are applied.

By the same token, you sometimes have to increase your reality's inertia to prevent forces you don't want from making changes you don't like.

Newton's Second Law of Motion: The alteration of motion is ever proportional to the motive force impressed, and is made in the direction of the right line in which that force is impressed.

A stronger force will *accelerate* an object (change its speed and/or direction) more than a weaker force will. When an object accelerates, it'll move in the direction determined by the combination of the forces pushing on it (the *resultant vector*). The greater the mass of the object, the more force it takes to change the state of its motion.

Here is the equation:

$F = a/m$
The force (F) is equal to the acceleration (a) divided by the mass (m).

Now that the object is in motion, does it still have inertia? You bet! Think about a giant ocean liner and a tiny speedboat, both going in the same direction at the same speed. What happens when they both try to turn? The small boat has far less mass than the big one, so it doesn't resist nearly as much and can change direction quickly. It's very difficult to get the large boat to turn, speed up, or slow down.

Second Magical Law of Motion: The acceleration of an individual or consensual perception is directly proportional to the net force acting upon it, is in the direction of the net force, and is inversely proportional to the strength (will) of the perception.

Here is the equation:

$a \propto F/p$
The change in direction (a) increases as the force (F) applied to it increases, and decreases as the target's perceptive will (p)— their resistance to change—increases.

The greater the inertia of the system, the more energy it will take to see a change. Consider, too, the element of *time*. I don't have room to show you more equations, but suffice it to say that the quicker you want results, the more force you have to use.

A positive affirmation that only affects your own perception of yourself (assuming your subconscious expectations are susceptible to change) is easier to pull off than a spell to create world peace, no matter how much everyone wants it (or says they do). The perspectives and expectations of six billion humans create an incredible mass with a formidable momentum.

Newton's Third Law of Motion: To every action there is always opposed an equal reaction; or the mutual actions of two bodies upon each other are always equal, and directed to contrary parts.

The more familiar paraphrase of this law is "For every action, there is an equal and opposite reaction."

When a force changes an object's state of rest or motion, the object resists that change, resulting in a force that pushes back with equal strength, in an opposite direction.

We don't detect this push when there's a great difference between the masses. If you hold a rock in the air, the earth's gravity is pulling down on it with a measurable force. But the rock's mass creates its own gravity, too. The difference between their masses is so large that we don't notice, but as the rock is pulled toward the earth, the earth is also pulled ever so slightly toward the rock.

Third Law of Magical Motion: Whenever one individual or consensual will exerts a force on a second individual or consensual will, the second perception exerts an equal and opposite force on the first.

Be aware of the energy you project, and the direction in which you project it, since you'll feel it push back when your energy collides with the mass and inertia of its target. This also means that if you want to overcome the inertia of reality, the force you project has to be greater than its ability to push back.

You may think that casting spells to get rich quick is a great idea, but if you can't muster the willpower to adjust your own expectations *and* act in accordance to increase the energy of the force you project *and* overcome the inertia of consensual reality (including others'

Fairness is a subjective construct, not an objectively definable variable. One person's unacceptable reality is someone else's paradise, and they'll exert all the force they can to prevent changes.

resistance to letting go of their money, especially those who have a huge mass of it), you're not going to get very far. In fact, the only detectable result you're likely to experience is the consensual backlash: a reinforcement of the reality in which everyone believes you should be grateful to slog away at a job, earning just enough to survive from day to day.

It doesn't seem fair, does it? No, but fairness is a subjective construct, not an objectively definable variable. One person's unacceptable reality is someone else's paradise, and they'll exert all the force they can to prevent changes. Even those who insist they're suffering often seem to choose unpleasant familiarity rather than adjust to a different reality.

Physics is just math, and while it may not be "fair," at least it's predictable. Learn how to use it to your advantage.

Setting Up Your Equations

Variables in magical equations are a lot fuzzier than their physical counterparts. Using the basic models can help you plan more effectively. When you want to change reality, whether through magic, activism, or just believing *really, really hard*, start with a clear definition of the results you're after, the types of forces you'll need to apply, and the best direction in which to apply them.

What are you trying to accomplish?

A billiards player doesn't smack random balls in random directions, expecting to win just because they want it badly enough. They're constantly evaluating the table, refining their strategy as the positions change over time, and calling each shot.

It takes a lot more force to break up the grouped balls at the beginning of the game (and the player has less control over the results) than it does to gently nudge the eight ball into the corner pocket for the win.

"World peace" sounds nice (as does "being a millionaire"), but you can't just teleport to the end goal, so break it down. How many different paths lead to the same destination? What are the smaller steps along these paths? Which of those steps do you have the best chance of controlling? Focus on those, one at a time.

Then evaluate the basic components of the system at each step.

What comprises the mass of the current system? What is its inertia like? Where are the weak points that can most easily be separated from the whole and pushed in a different direction?

Consider the inertial expectations and desires of everyone involved (including yourself), the myriad forces that affect their expectations and behavior at every moment, and the directions in which all these forces are already moving. Big changes that affect consensual reality take an unbelievable amount of energy, and it usually must be applied over a very long time.

To break up physical objects, societal traditions, and ingrained expectations and belief structures, sometimes you just have to make a mess at first and sow confusion. This may not initially have the effect you want, but it does make it easier to maneuver the individual parts, gradually accelerating the greater mass in the desired direction.

How much energy will it take for you to overcome the inertia? How can you increase the force you apply? How will the opposing forces push back?

Choosing the right spell components and astrological timing, keeping a journal to help spot patterns, working with other like-minded folks, and good old perseverance will increase the energy of the forces you're using to push a system along the path you choose.

Be aware, though, that everyone has goals, and many of those goals naturally work against yours, whether it's intended or not. You *might* be able to control random lotto numbers with magic, but how many others are also trying to push the odds in their favor? Resolving climate change is a great idea, but for everyone who still relies on industrial-age technology for daily necessities, that would mean huge, inconvenient changes to an established system. If we want to steer consensual reality in a better direction, our energy needs to be more powerful than its combined mass and all the forces pushing back on us.

I would personally love to live in a world where no one needs to pin their hopes for survival on random lotto numbers.

Let's get to work.

Rev. J. Variable x/ø *is currently pushing reality toward a system in which its lifelong passions for worldbuilding, fantasy role-playing games, and creating weird little art publications have combined to become a lucrative career, as the whole lotto thing never really panned out. This article is a revised excerpt from its upcoming book,* A Course in Somniscience. *Visit the portfolio at www.dreamsoverzero.com.*

Illustrator: Bri Hermanson

Open Your Mind: How to Add Cannabis to Your Spiritual Practice

Kerri Connor

Ritual. Spellwork. Meditation. All of these practices have many aspects in common, including the fact that by adding cannabis to them, they become even more powerful.

Religious traditions around the world have used cannabis for spiritual purposes for thousands of years. Support for the use of cannabis in neopagan traditions is on the rise.

In my practice, working with cannabis in a spiritual setting is no different than using other plant material, such as lavender buds or frankincense resins. All plants are a gift from our Mother Earth. We simply must learn how to use them.

Cannabis, like other altar items, other correspondences, or music, is a tool that can be used in several different ways. How you use it depends on your intention. What do you want cannabis to do for you?

- Do you want it to relieve stress from the day to put you in a more positive frame of mind before performing a working?

- Do you want to rip down your walls in a peak experience for a deep meditation in which you feel connected to the life force of the universe?

- Do you want to build energy to send out into the universe along with your magical intention?

- Do you want to draw down the moon or communicate one-on-one with your deities?

Cannabis is a tool that can help you do all these things and more. No matter how you want to use your cannabis, there are steps you can take to imbue it with your intention.

A Cache for Your Stash

The very first step in using cannabis in a spiritual manner is to treat it spiritually. Separate some of your bud out for spiritual use and keep it in a container separate from your medicinal or recreational stash.

Choose a container that speaks to you. You will eventually want several different containers, each dedicated to a specific purpose. Once you begin blessing your cannabis, you'll understand better the potential desire for several containers.

I personally use three different containers to store cannabis for spiritual use. My first box is a plexiglass chest with a locking clasp. I know, *plastic*—but it's see-through and works great for moon blessings and is far safer when I put it outside overnight on my deck, which is frequented by local wildlife, including opossums, raccoons, skunks, and a fox. After a moon blessing, the cannabis goes into one of two other boxes. One of those is a wood box with an engraved Om symbol. This is where I store and bless my meditation cannabis. The other is a wood box with the triple moon carved into the lid. This holds my moon-blessed cannabis until I am ready to use some to bless it with a more specific purpose. My plexiglass chest, then, can also double as a vessel to use when only blessing a small amount of cannabis.

Take some time to choose your containers. Don't just grab the closest thing. You want them to speak to you, to represent your beliefs, so put some effort into it. A clear container is preferable for full moon blessings so that the light of the moon is able to shine down upon your flower.

Now that I've introduced you to using different containers and separating your cannabis for different uses, let's discuss blessing cannabis for those uses.

Full Moon Blessing

All your cannabis can be blessed under the full moon. You can then portion it out to bless in other ways as desired.

To begin, simply place your cannabis in a see-through container and place in a safe location either outside under the full moon or in a window where the moon can "see" it. Before you set the container down, hold it in both hands, look up at the moon, and recite the following three times:

Moon above, with your glow,
Bless my flower with your power.

After the third time, remember to say thank you.

This is the easiest and simplest way to bless your cannabis, and it's also quite effective. It's very similar to making moon water. While you can use any full moon to bless your cannabis, you can also look to the moon for different correspondences. For example, the January full moon corresponds with new beginnings, so if you focus on the intent, cannabis blessed under the January full moon will help you deal with or initiate new beginnings.

Blessing Cannabis for Meditational Use

One of the greatest uses of cannabis in a spiritual manner is with your meditations. Using cannabis for meditation allows you to be more open with yourself. It helps calm the mind, ease anxiety, center and ground. It allows you to see things more objectively and to lower the walls your ego uses to protect yourself. Cannabis helps those meditate who have difficulty focusing or shutting their mind down. Mine likes to run nonstop. It's terrible. For years I would try meditation and I simply could not handle more than five minutes at a time (and it always felt like far longer than five minutes!). Once I began using cannabis medicinally, I quickly researched and learned about the spiritual benefits. Cannabis has helped me successfully add this important aspect to my practice.

Using cannabis for meditation allows you to be more open with yourself. It helps calm the mind, ease anxiety, center and ground. It allows you to see things more objectively and to lower the walls your ego uses to protect yourself.

Choose a container for your meditation cannabis and place it on your altar. Add a self-lighting charcoal tablet to a fireproof container. Sprinkle a combination of frankincense, lavender buds, and mugwort onto the tablet. Open your circle as you normally would.

Pass your container through the smoke as you visualize yourself deep in meditation: relaxed, otherworldly, ethereal. Imagine the qualities and skills you want to use while you meditate, for example, focus, patience, and acceptance. Are there issues you have with meditating? Visualize those issues disappearing. They are no longer a problem. They will no longer hold you back. Cannabis will allow you to perform your meditations as you need them to be performed in order to fully participate in them. Project your intentions into the flower you hold in your hand. Continue passing the container through the smoke. As you do, say:

> Bless this cannabis.
> Imbue it with your spirit.
> Lavender, grant me peace and aid my conscious mind.
> Frankincense, aid me in my meditations and deepen my spirituality.
> Mugwort, your powers for astral projection, clairvoyance, divination, dreams, and psychic abilities enhance my practice and take me to new realms.
> Bless this cannabis.
> Imbue it with your spirit.

If you work with a specific deity, you may ask them to bless your cannabis too by adding these words:

> (Deity), bless this cannabis with your grace, strength, and love.
> Imbue it with your spirit to guide me on my path.

Once your cannabis is blessed, it is ready to add to your meditation practice.

Blessing Cannabis for Specific Intentions

Every ritual or spell begins with an intention. You can bless your cannabis to correlate with any ritual or spell in order to incorporate it into your working. Your first step is to confirm your intention. Once you do, you will need to do some research to find elements that correspond with your intention. These elements can be herbs, oils, or even stones. *Llewellyn's Complete Book of Correspondences* by Sandra Kynes is a great reference tool. When using herbs or oils to bless your cannabis with your intention, the process is similar to the one for blessing it for meditation: using a fireproof container and charcoal tab, you will add the herbs and pass your flower through the smoke.

You will want to have your cannabis in another container to bless it. If you want to use stones, you can add those to your container to boost your intention. If you are only blessing a small amount for one-time use, you can even use your bowl, pipe, bong, joint, or whatever you use to consume your cannabis. You can also use something more creative, like a natural container such as a shell, or bowls carved from wood or dried gourds—anything you can safely add your cannabis to and then pass through smoke.

When you are prepared, add your herbs/oils to the lit charcoal tablet and pass your cannabis through the smoke. Focus on your intention and say:

> *Build my intention, strengthen my will.*
> *Allow the power this smoke radiates to permeate into these buds.*
> *Instill them with the virtues I seek.*
> *Bless them with your grace and energy to amplify my work.*

Your cannabis is now ready to use in your spellwork or ritual. It is especially beneficial to use cannabis when you do any type of spell or ritual that involves visualization, as it helps to boost the power.

Combining Herbs with Cannabis

One more way to boost the power of your workings is to combine cannabis with herbs that correspond to your intentions. Many herbs are smokable, but not all are, and some can make you very sick or worse, so be sure that what you are using is safe. Herbs you use for smoking should always be food grade and preferably organic. You can find many in the spice section in the baking aisle of your local grocery store, but some food-grade herbs (like lavender) generally have to be ordered online or bought at specialty shops, or you may be able to find them at some metaphysical shops. If you aren't sure if the herb is food grade, ask. If the store doesn't know, don't use it. Non-food-grade herbs may contain fertilizers or pesticides. Always be sure to verify it is food grade.

When working with herbs combined with your cannabis, you want to have more cannabis than herb. Generally, I use 70–90 percent cannabis, with the remaining 10–30 percent reserved for herbs. The percentage depends on what herbs you are using and your own personal taste. Lavender, which has a more mellow taste, is easy to use at 30 percent. Clove, on the other hand, is not. For clove, I use only 10 percent.

Combine your herb with your cannabis and place it on your altar. If you are using only a small amount at a time, you may bless it in your bowl or pipe or other device, or you can bless larger amounts in another type of container. If you do use a container, it sure wouldn't hurt to label it in some way so you always remember what herb you combined it with—particularly if you have several different stashes available to work from.

Because you are adding herbs to the cannabis, you do not need to pass them through smoke. Hold your hand over the mixture and say:

Bless this blend, created to _____ [state your intention].
As I consume this mixture,
As I inhale with each breath,
Bring me closer to my goal.
Bring me closer to my desires.
Bring me closer to my envisioned outcome.
So mote it be.

As you consume your blend, be sure to visualize your spell working in the intended manner.

. . . .

Cannabis is a powerful tool and should be treated with the respect and reverence it deserves. Always use caution and respect for cannabis in your spiritual workings and you will receive and experience the blessings from this truly remarkable and ancient plant.

Kerri Connor runs the Gathering Grove (a family-friendly, earth-based spiritual group) and has been practicing her craft for over thirty-five years. She is the author of seven books, including Wake, Bake & Meditate: Take Your Spiritual Practice to a Higher Level with Cannabis and 420 Meditations: Enhance Your Spiritual Practice with Cannabis. A graduate of the University of Wisconsin, Kerri earned a BA in communications. She is a cancer survivor and lives in Illinois with her husband, a son, three cats, and a plethora of critters. She is working to convert a portion of their land into a spiritual sanctuary. Visit her at www.KerriConnor.com.

Illustrator: M. Kathryn Thompson

Speak Little, Listen Much: Learning from Others at Every Stage of Practice

Thorn Mooney

There's a line in the "Rede of the Wiccae" by Gwen Thompson, first published in *Green Egg* magazine in 1975, that goes, "Soft of eye an light of touch—speak little, listen much." It's one of the most frequently quoted sections of the poem so often called the "long version" of the Wiccan Rede, and it's easy to see why. It's a worthwhile reminder that we often learn more and have deeper experiences when we do more listening than speaking.

Whether or not you identify as Wiccan, and whether or not the "Rede of the Wiccae" holds any special significance for

you, it's worth taking the time to contemplate this particular sentiment. As in the Four Powers of the Sphinx described by Eliphas Lévi and popularly known as the Witches' Pyramid—to know, to dare, to will, and to keep silent—we are advised yet again that in order to grow in the magical arts, we must cultivate wisdom in the quiet. In other words, if we want to grow as witches, we need to shut up and listen! Seems simple enough, right?

Well, yes and no. As witches and magicians, we're always listening and learning at every stage of our paths. But just because we're students doesn't mean we don't have lots to share as well. Reading books by yourself, studying with peers, sitting at the proverbial feet of community elders, attending workshops, and following blogs and social media accounts are all examples of listening to the wisdom of others. At some point in your path, you may find yourself on the other side of these roles—perhaps writing your own blogs and books, leading classes and covens, or organizing and teaching at events—but you won't ever hit a point where you've learned all there is to know and no longer need to occupy the student role. It just won't happen (even though at some point you might fall into the trap of mistaking boredom and stagnation for having learned it all, but more on that in a minute).

Sometimes in witchcraft communities, we talk about each other (and ourselves) as though we're only ever one or the other: a newbie or an experienced witch, a student or a teacher, a neophyte or an elder. Beginners listen and elders teach. It's not much of a jump from here to those old portrayals of mid-twentieth-century classrooms, where good children kept quiet and copied lines and never questioned adults. Contemporary classrooms don't run this way anymore. We know now how much children can learn by interacting with each other as well as their teachers, and the best classrooms are highly collaborative, with many of them focused on student-led education. I learned a lot from my own students when I worked in the classroom, and my teacher friends always said the same. Both teachers and students come with their own thoughts and experiences to share, and the relationship is mutually beneficial. This is no less true in educational spaces among witches.

We have the added advantage of not being children! That sounds obvious, but I think a lot of us lose sight of this critical reality when we start exploring the Craft, as well as when we start *teaching* for the first time. Too often I've been in discussions with my fellow coven leaders and someone will ask, "How do you make your students do X?" When I say, "I don't, because they're adults and I assume that if X is important to them, they will do it without me chasing them," it's sometimes treated as though I'm being needlessly provocative and don't understand that students *need* chasing and chastisement, that they *need* constant monitoring and prodding and regular reminders. But, in my experience, even adults who thrive in highly structured spaces and appreciate clear boundaries already have a handle on conducting themselves appropriately and keeping their lives in order. They don't need me to overstep my bounds and turn into a professor or parent.

Meanwhile, beginners sometimes give away just a little *too* much of their own power when they enter into learning environments, which could result in falling prey to abusive situations or else just tolerating a not-quite-right fit (be it a coven, a teacher, or a tradition) for longer than they should. Consider also the increasing popularity of the term *baby witch* online today. It's often meant endearingly, but sometimes it's tossed around as an insult and is used to imply that beginners can't make choices for themselves, can't think critically, or can't function without "adult" supervision and care.

But here's the thing: just because you're new to something doesn't mean you're new to *everything*. Just because someone is a student doesn't mean they don't have lots to share as well. This is something that a lot of beginners (and a lot of us experienced witches, too) don't always realize, and it's also one of the reasons why being a beginner sometimes feels so

In reality, "speak little, listen much" applies to all of us, whether we're brand-new witches or established elders with massive downlines and piles of books with our names on the spine. We all learn the most when we make space for each other and listen.

overwhelming. When we're first told to "keep silent" or "speak little," we take that to mean that we don't have the authority to question what we're being taught, that everyone who has been around longer than us is equally worth listening to, or even just that we don't already possess thoughts and experiences that can inform our practice of the Craft. And all of this is untrue!

In reality, "speak little, listen much" applies to all of us, whether we're brand-new witches or established elders with massive downlines and piles of books with our names on the spine. We all learn the most when we make space for each other and listen. So how do we ensure that we're always doing that? How do we make sure we're not falling into negative situations as we progress as witches?

Remember That We're All Students

I've been working as the high priestess of a traditional Wiccan coven for about seven years. That's not long, really, when you consider that there are people out there who've been active for decades. I still think of myself as a beginner! I struggle and I'm constantly asking others for input and advice. I worry about handling every situation that arises as well as possible, and I struggle sometimes with big questions about what it all means, what the gods want, and whether I'm doing it right.

That's just how my brain works (hello, anxiety!). I consciously have to stop, revisit my magical journals, and watch the progress of my initiates in order to appreciate how far I've come as both a witch and a priestess. Sometimes my own high priestess and high priest, or even one of my initiates, will point out to me the progress I've made. They all function as my teachers here. It's an incredible feeling, but what I want you to see here is that it isn't a particularly *automatic* one. It takes reflection and outside input. That's because I'm still a student!

Every stage we enter, we do so as a beginner. It never, ever stops. So take advantage of the many people around you (authors, online friends, your own students, covenmates, and really anyone who will hold still long enough) and allow them to teach you. This is especially important for long-term practitioners and practitioners on plateaus. It's not uncommon to eventually find yourself in a position where you feel like you've seen or read it all, but don't make the mistake of concluding that you've then *learned* it all. Often, the most creative and challenging ideas come from newcomers, who don't yet have the internal filters in place that inadvertently hinder their thinking.

Remember That We're All Autonomous, No Matter How Experienced We Are

This could be the very first book about witchcraft you've ever picked up. You could be brand-new to magic, to religion, to god work, to whatever. But you are *not* new at life. You are *not* new to critical thinking or discernment. Nobody ever has the right to your autonomy—not to your body, your decisions, your spirituality, your finances, or your personal power. You got that just by virtue of surviving up to this point (frankly, not an easy task). No matter how many traditions we're initiated into or how many books we've read or how many letters we have after our name, we are all human beings who are fundamentally entitled to respect.

You always have the right to walk away from a teacher (or a student), from a coven, from a tradition, from a toxic situation. And you don't need to justify that decision to anyone else. It doesn't even have to make *sense* to anyone else. Remembering this will shield you from a lot of the nastier stuff that sometimes happens in social settings, especially where power differentials are involved.

Now That You've Found Your Voice, Silence Is Still Sometimes the Best Approach

You always have a voice. You always have a right to your own ideas and opinions. (It's also always important that we speak up if we see something unjust in our communities.) However, when it comes to practicing witchcraft and magic, sometimes it really is the wisest choice to remain silent. The power to remain silent, as described by magicians and witches alike, isn't just about not talking and being sure to listen to others; it's also about the revelations and intangible shifts in your soul that happen in those spaces where you quiet your conscious mind and allow magic to work.

Some thoughts and experiences are for you alone. They won't make sense to other people because they're not *for* other people. For beginners, that means allowing yourself to have experiences that you don't offer up to other people for dissection. It means trusting your intuition and having the patience to sit with something without immediately asking, "But what could this mean?" For coven leaders and teachers, it means getting comfortable with the uncomfortable idea that maybe not everything you know needs to be passed on, beaten into a curriculum, or spelled out in plain language so no one gets it wrong. Gods and traditions have a way of guarding and preserving themselves, I've found. We don't need to burn ourselves out by making sure that all of our words get said.

All stages of the Craft—whatever type of Craft you may be practicing—pose their own challenges and offer their own rewards. We're all always learning, always a beginner at something, and always going to struggle sometimes. You probably won't even notice the transition from "beginner" to "experienced," simply because so many of us never stop feeling the weight of how much we don't know! Use this to cultivate compassion for others, wherever they are in their own explorations. Approach your interactions (with peers, teachers, or texts) with the assumption that the people involved have something to offer. You may be disappointed from time to time, but more often than not, you will be surprised and gratified at how much you can learn. Embrace whatever stage you're in, and remember that you, too, have a lot to teach.

Thorn Mooney *is a Gardnerian priestess operating in Raleigh, North Carolina. She is the author of* Traditional Wicca: A Seeker's Guide *and* The Witch's Path: Advancing Your Craft at Every Level *and has been blogging, sharing videos, and creating magical content online for more than a decade. Thorn holds graduate degrees in religious studies and English literature and works in academic publishing. Visit her online at www.thornthewitch.com and find her on Instagram @thornthewitch.*

Illustrator: Tim Foley

Magical Self-Care

Nurture Your Body, Mind & Spirit

Terrific Talismans: Empower Objects to Enhance Your Personal Space

A.C. Fisher Aldag

A talisman is a physical object used to hold and contain magickal power. Its energy is slowly released for a specific purpose. A talisman can be a single object, such as a horseshoe placed above the door, prongs up in a U-shape, which contains the quality of luck and protection for the household. A talisman can also be a collection of items, such as a cloth bag filled with healing crystals and herbs. These objects will "marinate" together, augmenting their energies. Sigils such as a pentagram or rune can be talismans as well. The physical objects

can be charged with natural forces, using words of power and ritualized actions, to imbue them with magickal capabilities.

Some practitioners use the words *talisman* and *amulet* interchangeably, yet I define an amulet as a power object that is worn by a person or animal. Some folks use the word *charm* for a physical item that contains energy, as in "a rabbit's foot is a lucky charm," but for my purposes, I define a charm as the spoken words used to "bespell," or empower, a talisman.

Talismans often have magickal properties of their own, like a four-leaf clover or a hagstone (a rock with a hole worn all the way through it by water). These objects do not require special ceremonies or words to fill them with energy. They are said to have an intrinsic power. However, most talismans need to be activated by voicing intent and by raising and focusing energy to store within the object.

Talismans can be ordinary household items, especially for traditional Witches or folk magick practitioners. Bent pins driven into windowsills, a sickle blade hidden within a chimney, or open scissors placed under the doormat repel baleful influences. Not only do bells on the doors announce visitors, but their sounds keep malicious beings from entering the home. A broom standing straws-up ensures that malign creatures must count every straw before entering. Hematite, which is magnetic, can remove negative influences.

> **Not only do bells on the doors announce visitors, but their sounds keep malicious beings from entering the home. A broom standing straws-up ensures that malign creatures must count every straw before entering.**

To attract beneficial beings and energies, colored bottles are placed on windowsills, catching sunlight and moonlight within. Mollusk shells in kitchen cupboards invite abundance. So do acorns with the cap intact, kept in a pocket or coin purse. Certain herbs hung from the rafters attract health and prosperity, such as Saint John's wort gathered on Midsummer, placed above the bedframe, with the flowers hanging down. Dried rose petals and a rose quartz crystal folded into a lacy handkerchief, or sewn into a pink velvet bag, summons love. Many of these items are readily available in nature or can be purchased at your local metaphysical shop.

Some Historic Talismans

In the British Isles and the US, anthropologists have discovered many historic talismans, including witch bottles, hidden clothing, protective amulets, and lucky pieces. Brass talismans adorned horses and wagons to ensure a safe journey. Witches in Cymru (Wales) collected the foot of a chicken or of a wild bird that had died naturally, then wrapped it around a crystal such as an agate or moonstone and used both to repel evil and to attract beneficial energies. The "hand of glory" in literature was an American mayapple or European mandrake root, wrapped around the fruit of that plant, then folded into one of its broad leaves and tied with black yarn.

In past days, people inscribed talismanic sigils on their possessions to repel malicious spirits. These sigils are called apotropaic marks, hex marks, or witch's marks. Symbols such as a mazy cross or daisy wheel were carved into fireplace mantels or beams of cottages and barns. The pentagram sigil of modern Wicca was traditionally used to protect a homestead. Symbols of the evil eye were painted on ships or worn as amulets to guard people from "bewitchment." Historians in Britain have actually begun to catalog these sigils, and have found over a thousand of them as of this writing.

Modern practitioners can use essential oil, water, chalk, or paint to create a temporary apotropaic mark. For example, drawing an image of a linchpin on your car's hubcaps ensures a safe journey.

Amulets

An amulet of a Christian cross, a Mjölnir (Thor's hammer), or a Wiccan pentacle can be used not only as a symbol of faith but also as a talisman for personal well-being. Jewels with protective powers include Scottish cairngorm (a variety of smoky quartz) and British jet. Small leather bags filled with a buckeye, a cat's shed claws, a rooster spur, a black tourmaline crystal, or a Rowan wood cross tied with red thread serve to protect individuals from illness or bad fortune. While amulets are most often worn as necklaces, they can also be brooches attached to clothing, old-fashioned watch chains, or hairpins. In past days, children were given a silver spoon at birth and wore bracelets made of amber beads to help them stay healthy and safe.

Creating Your Own Talismans

The best times to create talismans to attract a beneficial condition are during a new moon in the period from approximately Imbolc/Calan Fair/Candlemas (February 1–2) to Lammas/Lughnassadh/Harvesttide (August 1). For talismans to repel harmful entities, work during the dark or waning moon in the waning half of the year, especially around Hallowe'en/Samhain/Nos Calan Gaeaf or Yule/Winter Solstice/Alban Arthan. For optimal results, talismans can be charged on the full moon. The most fortuitous day of the week depends on the talisman's purpose. A protective amulet should be empowered on a Tuesday, using the martial qualities of Tyr or Mars. A talisman to attract love should be charged on a Friday, utilizing the loving energies of Freyja or Venus.

The rites to craft and charge a talisman can be performed during any esoteric working. Magickal practitioners may wish to establish a ritual protective space or shield themselves according to their own traditions.

The power object can be assembled and inscribed with esoteric sigils or with requirements written onto paper that is kept with the talisman. It is crucial to speak aloud your intent during this portion of the ceremony.

The power object can be assembled and inscribed with esoteric sigils or with requirements written onto paper that is kept with the talisman. It is crucial to speak aloud your intent during this portion of the ceremony, for example, "I ask that this black-thorn twig, tied with crow's feathers, will protect my desk from any thieves." Charming the talisman connects the physical item to its desired result.

Witches may invoke mag-ickal helpers, spirits, or deities and raise or draw power as they would for any other spell. However, instead of releasing the energy to travel where it will, it is directed into the talisman. Some practitioners use a wand, an athame, or a crystal point to guide power from the ether, or universal Source, into the object. Others raise their talisman in their palms toward the sky, then point it down toward the earth. It is also helpful to give the talisman a specific time limit, for instance, "This bag of crystals will keep me healthy all winter." The object will then slowly release the force in small increments, like a time-release capsule.

Talismans created during the sabbats can last for the six-week interim between traditional seasonal holidays. The objects can take on the ener-gies of a natural event. Examples include Brigid's crosses for Imbolc; oak, ash, and thorn boughs tied with red ribbon for Midsummer; corn dollies or wheat weavings for Lammas; and sprigs of holly, ivy, and mistletoe for Yule. "Power bags" of herbs, crystals, and other magickal items can be assembled during any gathering. The power raised during a bonfire or circle dance can infuse talismans with energy.

Cleansing and Disposing of Talismans

Permanent talismans, like an apotropaic mark carved into a doorway or an amulet that is worn often, must be periodically cleansed of accumulated energies. Talismans can be cleaned during the dark of the moon by asperging them with water droplets or smoke-cleansing them with burning sage, hazel withes, or all-purpose incense such as dragon's blood. Permanent talismans should also be periodically recharged, imbuing them with fresh magickal energy. The best time to recharge a power object is during a natural event, such as the full moon or a sabbat.

Some talismans, especially seasonal creations or those made for a specific purpose, will eventually lose their power and should be disposed of. Old power objects can be composted or ceremonially burned if none of their ingredients are harmful to the environment. If the talisman absolutely must be discarded with the trash, take it apart before putting it into the garbage bin so as not to harm custodians. Optimal times to get rid of worn-out talismans are Samhain, during the Yuletide/Winter Solstice season, or when hearth fires are extinguished and rekindled, like at Beltane. Talismans can also be discarded during a dark or waning moon in the waning half of the year.

Talismanic Spells

For home protection, obtain a piece of plaid cloth in dark colors, like navy blue and forest green. Baleful entities will have to count all of the squares, and can get lost within the pattern. Cut the fabric into a circle approximately six inches across. Place five protective items in the center of the cloth, such as the herb rue, a small black stone, an iron nail, a metal key, and a thorn from a hawthorn tree. Have a length of black thread on hand.

Prepare for magick according to your tradition, such as by casting a ritual circle. Speak your intent as you pull the edges of the fabric together to hold the objects. Bind the pouch with the black thread three times around, winding clockwise to close the opening, and tie it with a square knot. Summon power as you envision your home being a safe, comfortable sanctuary for you and your loved ones. Charge your talisman with energy. Hang this object from a window, saying as you do, "Only the blessed can enter."

"Cleopatra's needle" is an obelisk-shaped crystal in a container of earth, such as a flowerpot. Use local dirt or sand rather than soil bought from a garden store. The crystal can be plain quartz, but black tourmaline, obsidian, or cairngorm (smoky quartz) works the best. Charge the talisman with intent. This power object acts as a lightning rod, attracting harmful energies to the crystal and then earthing them. Change the soil every so often, dumping out the old earth onto the ground.

• • • • • • • • • • • •

Talismans cannot prevent all bad things from happening, but they can help to safeguard people and animals, places such as homes and offices, and things like vehicles and work tools. Creating and charging talismans can be a wonderful part of your magickal practice. To find out more about talismans used in folk magick, please read my book *Common Magick: Origins and Practices of British Folk Magick*.

A.C. Fisher Aldag (*Bangor, Michigan*) *has practiced a folk magico-religion from the British Isles for over forty years. She has assisted in facilitating many local Pagan events and regularly teaches classes and workshops on folk magick. Her book* Common Magick: Origins and Practices of British Folk Magick *is available from Llewellyn.*

Illustrator: Rik Olson

Salt, Sage & Self-Care: A Little Magical Pampering Goes a Long Way

Charlie Rainbow Wolf

Self-care. What does it mean? Why is it important? Most importantly, how can you make time for it in the middle of a hectic schedule?

I struggled trying to find the right terminology for this article. Self-centered. Self-care. Self-indulgent. Self-absorbed. Why do all these terms beginning with *self* have such a negative connotation?

You are yourself. You cannot be anything else, no matter how hard you try. Even though our twenty-first-century society might be trying to tell you that being selfish or self-indulgent or any of these other self-starting words is a bad thing, I beg to differ. *If you don't look after yourself, how can you look after anyone else?*

So how do you take care of yourself while avoiding the negative connotation of being elitist or narcissistic? The answer is by not falling into the trap of thinking you are greater or lesser than anyone else. If you are going to really care for others in your life, then taking time out to recharge your batteries and look after yourself is not self-indulgent or selfish or self-centered—it's necessary.

What Is Self-Care?

Picture this scenario. You've had a busy week at work, and perhaps you've brought work home to do, or maybe you even work from home rather than commuting. Your calendar is full of social engagements and appointments and to-do lists.

If you're anything like I used to be, the first thing you cancel to make more time (which is an illusion—time is something that either you have or you don't; it cannot be created) is your fitness session or your morning walk or the afternoon you planned to spend doing a favorite hobby. Meal prep becomes a hurried reheat of something from a box or packet rather than the full recipe you intended to make. If finances are a bit short, it's the book you wanted to read or the shoes you were saving for that get shoved aside.

I've noticed that as the speed of life increases, it's self-care that suffers. Sometimes it takes a wake-up call to turn things around. For me, it was a broken arm. I was lucky; for others, it's something much more serious.

Self-care starts with the confidence to say no. "I'd love to come to your party, but no, I can't make it." "I'm thankful to be offered the overtime, but no, I must respectfully decline." "I want to watch the movie with you, just not tonight, but most definitely another time."

Saying no is empowering. It's the first step in self-care, for it not only displays confidence but also establishes boundaries. Inanimate objects cannot say no; they're used whenever they're needed or desired. Saying no establishes your identity and is the start to recognizing your worth.

Self-care is a responsibility. I can feel some of you tensing up even as I write these words. You might want to argue that paying the bills, fixing the lamp, going to the dentist, or making the car payment is also your responsibility. You would, of course, be absolutely right—but how can you do any of those things if you're burned out because you neglected your self-care?

Before my broken arm, I was the queen of list making, and I would cram every minute of every hour of every day full of something. I felt I had no value if I wasn't being productive—which, of course, is absolute hogwash. The universe kept sending me signs to slow down, but I didn't listen. Only when I broke my arm and was severely restricted (because of the placement of the fracture) did I start to reevaluate things.

At first I was quite despondent and very angry and frustrated. "Why did this have to happen?!" Then my friend reminded me that her late mother would sit several times a day with a glass of tea and a cigarette and do nothing but relax and ruminate. It made me recall my mum doing the same thing, sitting with a cup of coffee and the morning newspaper. Why is taking time to unwind throughout the day (seemingly) a thing of the past?

Little things—a hot cup of tea, watching the rain course down a glass pane, a nice hot shower, a walk through nature—are simple

> **Saying no is empowering. It's the first step in self-care, for it not only displays confidence but also establishes boundaries.**

yet crucial for your happiness, peace of mind, and health. Self-care isn't just doing things that make you feel better; it's doing things to make you a better person.

Start Simple with a Foot Soak

Simple self-care starts with devoting a bit of time to yourself and then sticking to the plan. Keeping that promise to yourself is just as important as keeping a vow made to someone else—perhaps even more so. It doesn't have to be expensive, either.

One of my favorite things to do at the end of a long, busy day is a simple salt foot soak. I like this because I can multitask while I'm doing it, whether it's going through the mail or sorting out a knitting pattern or making a shopping list. A foot soak is easy and inexpensive and doesn't take a lot of time, yet because it's not part of a routine—like brushing my teeth, for example—it feels like a bit of an indulgence. It's also hard to run around and do chores when my feet are in a tub of water!

SALT FOOT SOAK

- 1 ½ cups Epsom salt

- ¾ cup sea salt

- ¼ cup additional salt (Dead Sea, Himalayan, etc.)

- 1 tablespoon herbal blend or a few drops of your favorite essential oil

Mix the ingredients together thoroughly in a large bowl. I prefer glass over plastic, but use what is available. It won't impact the outcome. Store the blend in an airtight container. Again, I prefer glass, and a colored glass seems to work best, but if only a plastic jar is handy, that will indeed work.

This recipe makes over 2 cups of herbal salts, which is easily enough for six to eight foot soaks. I use about ⅓ cup salts to a gallon of warm water. I've used both dry herbs and essential oils with this, and I've learned from experience that the herbs seem to work the best. Sometimes if the soak is not used when it is fresh, it will cake together if oils have been added. This doesn't impact its usefulness in the foot soak (it will still dissolve), but it does make it hard to get out of the storage jar!

If essential oils are included, consider keeping them separate from the salts and add them to the foot soak with the water. Be sure to use pure essential oils rather than fragrance oils, as some fragrance oils are full of artificial additives that are not suitable for bath and body products. They also don't impart the same magical energies as real essential oils do.

The herbs you choose are important here, for some are invigorating and some promote relaxation. It all depends on what the foot soak is meant to do. Personally, I like the relaxing herbs, and my favorites are sage, rosemary, and lavender.

Bath Salts

It's only a hop from a foot soak to bath salts. (See what I did there?) It's the same principle and the same basic recipe, although you'll need more because a bathtub holds more water than a tub used with a foot soak. The one caution I would make here is to remember that the feet are more resilient than the skin on the more delicate parts of the body, so make sure that any herbs or essential oils used won't cause any discomfort. I learned this the hard way with peppermint oil!

There's something magical about a long, luxurious soak in a tub full of soothing salts and opulent oils. To make it really enchanting, safely light some relaxing candles and add a few of your treasured crystals. Put on some relaxing music and prepare a favorite beverage. There's a reason for all of this.

Sentient beings experience everything through their five senses. When we experience relaxation on all levels—touch, smell, sight, sound, taste—not only does it feel gratifying, but the body's entire energy field is affected. The subtle body as well as the physical body are pampered, and both the physical and the etheric energy signatures are brought back into balance.

My go-to recommendations for bath salts are always those that are relaxing and soothing. For herbs, I use catmint, chamomile, lavender, rosemary, sage, and sometimes ginger. (Just a pinch of ginger is a really good additive when it's cold or when you're feeling under the weather.) To the foot soak recipe, I often add Celtic sea salt. I like to think that it takes me away to distant shores and forgotten times, but that might just be a flight of fancy.

It's possible to turn these salts into bath bombs, if something fizzy is desired. Bath bombs are fun to make but are often quite messy. In addition to the actual ingredients, a mold to shape them is needed. I recommend starting simple with a basic half-globe mold, but all shapes and sizes of cavities are available from craft suppliers and soap-crafting shops.

Bath Bomb

- ½ cup Epsom salt

- 1 cup baking soda

- ½ cup citric acid

- ½ cup cornstarch

- Coloring pigment, if desired (I have added Brazilian clay with good results.)

- 2 tablespoons carrier oil (I prefer jojoba, but warmed coconut oil works really well, too.)

- A few drops of water

- A few drops of your favorite essential oil

Mix all of the dry ingredients together in a large bowl. Again, I prefer glass over plastic. Add any color of pigment at this time, as this will be the final color of the bath bomb. Mix all of the wet additives in a separate small bowl. The wet ingredients must be combined with the dry ones ever so slowly, or the citric acid will start fizzing.

Once the mixture is combined, keep working with it until it resembles wet sand. Fill both halves of the bath bomb mold, packing the mixture in tightly until each part is slightly too full. Then press the two parts of the mold together firmly. Let it sit for at least two minutes, then gently tap the mold and pull the two halves apart. If it all goes to plan, the mold will come away from the bath bomb and can then be reused. Just be aware that this does not always go as planned—and that is why I tend to work with bath salts rather than bath bombs. There's a skill in getting the texture of the mix right!

Shower Soaks

I once jokingly referred to shower soaks as "alternative incense," and it stuck. The way the steam swirls around me in the shower reminds me of the way the incense smoke swirls around me during my morning devotions. A shower soak is very handy when there is no access to a bathtub—or where any kind of smoking is prohibited, for that matter.

Both the foot soak and the bath bomb recipe can be used in the shower. There isn't the same level of relaxation as with a luxurious bath, but all of the magical elements are still there. I've found a shower soak to be most useful when I'm away from home and a bath is not ideal and it's impossible to burn herbs for a cleansing incense.

Using the same recipe for the foot soak or the bath salts, take ⅓ cup salts and place in the bottom of the shower. Do this after entering; it's more comfortable underfoot this way. As the hot water dissolves the salts, the steam will lift and disperse the soothing aromas from the herbs and oils. I'm particularly fond of doing this in the winter months, because not only is it relaxing but it also helps with winter colds.

The Herbs

Although I briefly touched on the herbs I like to use in my salts, I want to provide a more informative and in-depth review of some of my favorites. There are many ways of choosing which herbs to include in the recipes. For example, you might want to honor the energies of a particular Moon phase or Sun sign, or maybe your soak or shower is a precursor to a magical rite or ceremony. All of this and more will enhance your soaks and showers and make them more meaningful.

SAGE (*SALVIA OFFICINALIS*)

Sage has been my main go-to herb for well over two decades. Common garden sage has a wonderfully sweet smell when burned, and it's been suggested that sage can help rid the air of harmful bacteria. This herb is ruled by Jupiter and is aligned with the element of air. It is one of my signature herbs and goes in all of my foot soaks, bath salts, incense blends, and candles.

This is not to be confused with white sage (*Salvia apiana*), the sort seen bundled for use in smudging. White sage is native to the American Southwest and is an important plant to the indigenous people there. I used to use it regularly, but it has gained so much popularity that wild harvested *Salvia apiana* is at risk of becoming endangered. Because of this, I now urge people to only use cultivated white sage and to look at how they are using it. I've swapped to common garden sage for precisely that reason.

Common sage is easy to grow, and I think it adds to the magic when using herbs I have grown myself. Sage is valuable in soaks and smokes because it is said to promote long life and wisdom. In herbal remedies, sage helps to break up catarrh and mucus. It's a great herb to add to your soaks when feeling down in the dumps, because sage has long been used to lift the spirits.

Rosemary (*Salvia rosmarinus*)

This is the second of my go-to herbs for soaks and incense and other herbal blends. Rosemary is part of the same family as common sage but has a very different smell and taste. Until 2017 it was known as *Rosmarinus officinalis*. Like sage, rosemary has a sweet and earthy scent when burned, and when used in bath products, it brings the element of fire, for it is ruled by the Sun.

Rosemary is not difficult to grow and is a very attractive plant in the garden, but it does not like cold or wet feet. It can be a bit temperamental if the soil is too wet, and some cultivars are susceptible to frost. Rosemary was sacred to the Romans and Greeks, and the Egyptians used it as one of their embalming herbs. It's little wonder that rosemary is frequently used as a symbol of remembrance. Shakespeare even explicitly mentions rosemary in *Hamlet* and *The Winter's Tale*!

On a magical note, use rosemary in a soak to attract protection and purification. Rosemary is known to both stimulate the mind and promote sleep, and a rosemary soak or shower is a great way to try to incubate a dream or to help remember dreams upon awakening. Rosemary is also said to attract favorable attention, and is good to use before attending a job interview or meeting influential people.

LAVENDER (*LAVANDULA*)

Lavender is the third of my signature herbs, and again, I tend to include it in nearly every soak and incense I make. I remember being a young child and tying lavender in organza ruffles to make drawer sachets for Christmas gifts. Like rosemary and sage, lavender is a member of the mint family, *Lamiaceae*. It is associated with the element of air and is aligned with the planet Mercury.

Given the right conditions, lavender will grow prolifically. It's a great pollinator in the garden, and I've often grown it among fruit trees. It likes both nutritionally poor and well-drained soil, but will not survive harsh, freezing winters. Around the house, lavender has long been used to deter moths and other pests. It's use as a bath additive dates back to ancient Roman soldiers, who used lavender when washing themselves and their clothing.

For magical purposes, lavender is healing and relaxing, soothing and calming. I use it in relaxing salts and soaps and also in dream pillows to help incubate a good night's sleep. A long soak in a lavender bath is soothing to both the skin and the mind; lavender is known to bring relief to minor skin irritations and is used in aromatherapy to ease stress and tension. It is a purification herb as well as one that, like rosemary, helps to sharpen the mind and attract positive attention.

Conclusion

Of course, this is only the tip of the iceberg. There are many other ways to incorporate herbs into a relaxing routine. One of my favorite ways to use herbs is to add them to soap, for soap is something I use on a daily basis, and something frequently taken for granted. Every time I pick up the bar of soap, I see the herbs and say a quick prayer (I call them "prayer darts," as they're short, sharp, and to the point) to ignite the magical energies. This is an easy way to take a basic self-care routine and elevate it to have a magical purpose.

Once you're in the habit of self-care, it's easy to find time to devote to looking after yourself. There is nothing wrong with indulging in a little time to yourself, and there is nothing arrogant or narcissistic about wanting to be the best you can be; that is how you can offer the best of yourself to others. Take time now to make time for yourself. When you love yourself enough to look after yourself properly, and when you believe in yourself enough to take the time to make sure your own needs are met, that is when the real magic begins.

Further Reading

Cunningham, Scott. *Cunningham's Encyclopedia of Magical Herbs*. St. Paul, MN: Llewellyn, 1985.

Family Traditions. *The Bath and Body Book: DIY Bath Bombs, Bath Salts, Body Butter and Body Scrubs*. CreateSpace, 2014.

Soak, Olivia. *Recipes with Epsom Salts: Homemade Bath Salt Recipes with Essential Oils*. Published independently, 2016.

White, Lorraine. *How to Make Bath Bombs, Bath Salts & Bubble Baths: 53 All Natural Recipes*. CreateSpace, 2014.

Charlie Rainbow Wolf *is happiest when she's creating something, especially if it's made from items that others have discarded. Pottery, writing, knitting, astrology, and tarot ignite her passion, but she happily confesses she's easily distracted—life offers such wonderful things to explore! A recorded singer-songwriter and published author, she champions holistic living and lives in the Midwest with her husband and special-needs Great Danes. Astrology and tarot reports, handmade incense pots, herbs and herbal spellwork, and other accoutrements are available through her website at www.charlierainbow.com.*

Illustrator: Bri Hermanson

Cord Cutting: Ending Lingering Attachments

Emily Carlin

No person is an island, so the saying goes. Our lives are made up of multiple connections to other people—be they friends, family, coworkers, acquaintances, or lovers. Each of these personal connections creates a metaphysical cord that ties us to one another. For the most part, these cords take care of themselves, coming into being with the relationship and fading away when people drift apart. Unfortunately, sometimes cords remain strong long after the relationship has ended or become unhealthy. These lingering cords must be deliberately cut to allow both parties to heal and move forward.

What Are Cords?

Cords are the metaphysical threads that form between people in relationships that allow for an easy energetic exchange between them. When two people meet, their energetic bodies interact, exchanging small packets of energy as a matter of course. It's the metaphysical equivalent of smelling each other's perfume. As we develop relationships with others, our energetic bodies begin to recognize and naturally reach out to each other, exchanging increasing amounts of energy with growing ease. Over time, whether we want them to or not, these exchanges form a more permanent bond in the form of a metaphysical cord. These cords allow us to easily exchange energies and deepen our bonds.

Depending on the nature of the relationship, these cords can be beneficial or destructive. A beneficial cord promotes a sense of connection and belonging in a relationship. It can promote empathy and understanding by allowing the people involved to gently feel each other's energies. If you've ever felt so close to someone that they feel like an extension of yourself rather than a separate being, then you've experienced a robustly healthy cord. Unfortunately, cords can be just as harmful in a toxic relationship as they are beneficial in a healthy one. Cords promote closeness between people, and some people are not good for each other. Energetic ties to a domineering boss or an abusive partner can make people feel trapped in a bad situation and drain their energy. Thankfully, since cords are formed through energetic exchange and most people tend to avoid people who harm them, negative cords are less common than positive ones.

Cords can be of varying strengths, depending on the intensity of the attachment people have to one another. A weak cord is a frail and fragile thing, easily made and easily broken, with very little energy flowing through it. Think of the person you meet at a networking event whom you exchange business cards with and offer to meet for coffee, even though neither of you really intends to follow up. This creates a weak

cord that will fade quickly. If a weak cord is a single easily-snappable thread, then a strong cord is a thickly woven rope that firmly binds the people at either end. Think of your best friend, someone you've known for years and with whom you've gone through thick and thin. This is the kind of relationship that creates a robust cord, one that gives the people involved an intuitive sense of each other and a deep need for each other's presence. If you've ever felt an undeniable pull to call or visit a loved one, only to find that they've been thinking about you all day, then you've experienced the pull of a strong cord.

In the best scenarios, cords come into being as people become friendly with each other at the same pace and gently fade out as the relationship weakens equally. However, emotions are messy things and relationships are rarely perfectly equal. Just as one person can be more invested in a relationship than another, so can one person push more energy into a cord than another. Most of the time the imbalance will correct itself naturally, with both parties shifting to inputting equal amounts of energy. However, if the relationship is particularly unhealthy, it can lead to feelings of discomfort and paranoia. At worst, a strong unhealthy cord can lead to obsession or even stalking. Most imbalanced cords never have such an extreme impact, only becoming problematic if one person tries to hang on to the relationship when the other tries to walk away.

Problematic Cords

Like relationships, cords can be positive, negative, or problematic. It's easy to choose to nurture positive cords and to want to rid yourself of negative ones. For now, let's take a look at the more complicated case of a problematic cord. These are the cords of relationships that have their ups and downs, but perhaps there's a bit more negative than positive; these are the relationships that are imbalanced and where code-pendency or toxicity are mild but are likely to grow. There are a whole host of reasons why a person might want to hang on to a problematic relationship and thus not cut its cord.

In this case, throttling down the cord is the best course of action. Just as we throttle down a car to slow it down, we can reduce the amount of energy that can flow through a cord to lessen its effects. This reduces the negative effects of the cord while not completely severing the relationship; the energetic throttle (explained below) is the metaphysical component of a healthy set of boundaries. Further, it creates a sense of distance between you and the relationship, which will allow you to evaluate the situation with greater objectivity. Once you've throttled down the cord, you can more easily decide how you wish to proceed.

How to Throttle Down a Cord

Throttling down a cord can be accomplished through visualization. In your mind's eye, envision yourself and the other person standing in an empty room. Envision a glowing beam of energy, rooted in the solar plexus, flowing between the two of you. Take note of the width of the beam. Now envision a clamp in your hands. (The size and strength of the clamp should be proportional to the width and strength of the beam.) Take the clamp and attach it to the beam, tightening until the beam has narrowed sufficiently. This will reduce the amount of energy that can flow through the cord. You will need to repeat this exercise daily until the cord stabilizes at the strength you desire.

Cord Cutting

A negative cord or one that lingers past its time can trap people in toxic relationships. To release them, a cord cutting should be performed. However, there are consequences that must be considered before doing so. Cord cutting is a permanent act. Severing the metaphysical cord between two people severely limits the energy they can exchange, creating a sense of distance that usually leads to a feeling of extreme indifference toward the other person. If you wish to have any future relationship with the person beyond "indifferent acquaintance," then cord cutting might not be the best choice.

Cord cutting is most effective when you can truly separate yourself from the other person once the ritual is complete. It is critical to be mentally and emotionally committed to completely severing your relationship when you cut the cord, as a lingering desire to sustain the relationship can weaken the effectiveness of your ritual. Continued interaction with the other person can also weaken your working because of how easy it can be to fall back into familiar behaviors and energy flows. In a perfect world, you would perform a cord-cutting ritual and then never interact with that person again, allowing the relationship's energies to settle without outside interference. Low levels of interaction are usually fine so long as you remain committed to not exchanging energy. Continued interaction is problematic because accustomed energy patterns can be easily triggered. A strong will can

Cord cutting is most effective when you can truly separate yourself from the other person once the ritual is complete. It is critical to be mentally and emotionally committed to completely severing your relationship when you cut the cord, as a lingering desire to sustain the relationship can weaken the effectiveness of your ritual.

help you remain detached and minimize the energy exchange in such a situation; however, it will be far easier if you can avoid triggering old patterns in the first place.

Of course, we don't live in a perfect world and some people cannot be avoided. We may wish to cut a cord with a coworker, family member, or member of our greater community. Despite ending a personal relationship, these people will often be in our immediate area. For such unavoidable people, it may be better to simply throttle down the cord to its bare minimum and shield yourself to the best of your ability. If you do feel the need to cut such a cord, you will need to be extremely diligent in minimizing your interactions with the other person, or you risk falling into previous habits and undoing your work. Support from friends and metaphysical allies can help you maintain your resolve.

Once you've considered the supporting actions you'll need to take and the possible consequences, it's time to perform a cord-cutting ritual.

Cord-Cutting Ritual

Once you've decided to permanently end an attachment, you can perform a cord-cutting ritual. You must be fully committed, mentally and emotionally, to ending the attachment for the ritual to be effective. Any lingering doubts or hopes for rekindling the relationship will work against your efforts and undermine the magick.

This ritual can be done alone or with supportive allies. Cord cutting can be an intense emotional experience, so having a friend in the room or ready on speed dial can be highly beneficial. You will need:

• A blank sheet of paper and a writing instrument

• Materials for making a poppet: This can be as simple as two sheets of paper cut in the shape of a person and stapled together or as complex as a hand-sewn cloth doll. The poppet will be burned or buried, so be sure to use nontoxic materials.

- A 4-to-5-foot length of twine

- A cutting instrument (e.g., scissors or a sharp knife)

- A safe place to burn or bury the poppet

Take a moment to ground and center yourself. Create sacred space for your working using your preferred method, and invite any magickal allies you choose.

Think about the attachment you will end. On the piece of paper, write down the negative aspects of the relationship. Include the bad times, disappointments, slights, and harm that was caused. Allow your negative emotions to pour out into your written words. Take your time and allow yourself to experience your emotional journey.

When you're ready, make your poppet. On the head of the poppet, write the name of the person(s) who is on the other end of the cord. Take the paper on which you just wrote and tear it into pieces, then use them to stuff the doll.

Get the twine and tie one end around the waist of the poppet and the other around your own waist. This twine signifies the metaphysical cord between the two of you.

Hold the twine in your left hand and your cutting instrument in your right hand (or the reverse if you're left-handed). In a firm voice, say:

This relationship is over. (Other person's name) and I are toxic to each other. I return any fragments of their self that have been given to me and reclaim any fragments of myself that I have given to them. From this day forth, no energy will be exchanged between us. As I cut this cord, so do I permanently sever our connection.

Cut the cord and say:

We are separate and whole.

Allow yourself a few moments to experience any emotions this process may produce. Untie the twine from your waist and place it with the poppet. If you can safely burn the poppet while in sacred space, do so now. Otherwise, place it on the floor and burn or bury it once the ritual is over.

Take a moment to thank any allies you've called and then dispel your sacred space. Dispose of the poppet if you weren't able to burn it in ritual space.

After the ritual, be sure to engage in some self-care: take a cleansing bath, eat a nice meal, read a favorite story, etc. Cord cutting can be draining work, and it's worth taking some time to regenerate positive energies.

Final Words

Cord cutting is a powerful tool for releasing ourselves from unhealthy attachments. To obtain the best results, we must examine our relationships and determine if we want them to persist and how. When we are certain a relationship is no longer beneficial, we can end it definitively by severing its cord. Supported by mundane commitment, cord cutting will bring closure and end lingering attachments, allowing both parties to move on and become whole.

Emily Carlin *is a Witch, writer, teacher, and mediator based in Seattle. She currently teaches one-on-one online and at in-person events on the West Coast. During her twenty-plus years of practice, she has published articles on defensive magick, pop-culture magick, Santa Muerte, general Witchcraft, and more. For more information, visit http://www.e-carlin.com.*

Illustrator: M. Kathryn Thompson

Gemstones & Minerals for Self-Improvement

Devin Hunter

For many witches, gemstones and crystals are cherished partners in magic. They are our allies in spellcraft, our guardians against unwanted energies, and our companions along the ever-winding road of mysticism. When a witch finds themselves with a connection to one, there is often little that can be done to separate them from their crystalline comrades. We love our stones, and for good reason: they help us become better at what we do.

Working with gemstones and crystals in spells can be a rewarding experience, but when we turn the lens inward,

we find that our mineral allies are also capable of helping us manifest great change in our lives. Instead of asking, "What crystal(s) do I need for this spell?" try thinking, "What crystal(s) can help me build the life I want?"

Similar to how vitamins work in the physical body, crystals provide supplemental energy to our etheric body as well as to the etheric energy within the space they immediately occupy. Think of them as little transponders, constantly sending out psychic energy that can be either molded or directed. When we make the focus of our work ourselves, we are able to partner with the energies found within a stone to bring clarity, insight, and healing to all areas of our lives.

The work of self-improvement is a never-ending journey for all of us. It is hard to face our shadow, make a plan for forward motion, and make peace with the way things are—all of which are vital for growth and empowerment. For many of us, knowing where to be, how to proceed, and even what to do can be as daunting as climbing a mountain, but it needn't be. Crystals can help take the guesswork, anxiety, and fear out of self-improvement.

Choosing a Stone for Self-Improvement

There are some stones that come preprogrammed by nature to bring vast change through subtle adjustments. These are the stones that, simply by tapping into their frequency, will automatically harmonize with your vibration and begin their work without the need for programming (i.e., setting an intention for a stone). When you do actively program them, the benefits are enhanced exponentially.

Generally, any stone that you feel a connection with has some form of energy that you are craving. While not all stones readily lend their energy to humans, the five sisters of the quartz family are progressive in their approach to humanity. There are more than five stones in the quartz family, but these particular ones are usually willing allies.

CLEAR QUARTZ

Believed to be the most abundant crystal on earth, clear quartz brings clarity to every situation and helps us assimilate the information we receive into workable data. It essentially helps us make sense of life and provides opportunities for meaningful inner dialogue and spiritual growth. Are you unsure what to do about your job or finding it difficult to focus during meditation? This is the crystal for you! When it comes to sorting things out or finding the best way forward, few stones can assist us like clear quartz.

AMETHYST

Amethyst is beloved the world over for its beauty and its connection to humanity. In particular, it is known for assisting in the breaking of bad habits and addictions and is frequently gifted to those in recovery. This connection likely stems from its use by pirates as a tool to keep them sober during long voyages. Clean water was rare on the high seas, but apparently not rum! If you find yourself struggling with repetitive cycles, addiction, or self-sabotage, amethyst has your back. It is also known for assisting in the development of psychic abilities and intuition, both of which come in handy in the work of self-improvement.

ROSE QUARTZ

Most commonly known as a stone with the power to enhance love, rose quartz is highly sought after the world over. Unlike other stones that deal with love, it focuses specifically on self-love and sovereignty, two major factors in healing damage that has been done to the heart. This is a great stone to work with if you are in transition, as it guides you to make decisions that are in your best interest rather than from a place of dark emotion. Rose quartz helps you put your needs squarely in the center of your focus so that real, unconditional love can be both given and received.

Citrine

One of only a handful of self-cleansing stones, citrine is capable of bringing deep insight to any matter, especially where money is concerned. It is known as a stone of commerce and is often included in money magic. While citrine is useful in short-term acts of magic, like a quick money spell to get you through until payday, its ability to help with finances is actually much broader. Long-term planning and investments thrive under the watchful eye of citrine, as it helps us navigate the world of money and find ways to make changes for optimal growth. It is also the stone I recommend to people who are either afraid of or new to financial responsibility. Work with citrine in meditation before any big financial decisions and tune into it daily when you are actively manifesting financial change.

> **One of only a handful of self-cleansing stones, citrine is capable of bringing deep insight to any matter, especially where money is concerned.**

Smokey Quartz

Dark and mysterious, smokey quartz is a powerful ally to work with on our path as witches, lending guidance in matters of spiritual direction, gnosis, and discipline. Incredibly protective, it is often part of a spirit-worker's collection as a remedy for unwanted psychic energy and spiritual attention. Smokey quartz is known to help with recall during dreamtime and assist with astral travel. Overall, this makes it an excellent stone to work with when you are trying to figure out what to do next on your path. Work with it in meditation before ritual to reveal deep insights and after ritual to remove unwanted energies.

Choosing a Stone with Astrology

When choosing a stone, I also recommend the astro-method, which pairs you with a stone based on your astrological strengths and weaknesses according to your birth chart. Each chart comes with an elemental breakdown, which tells you how many planets in your chart are associated with each of the four elements, based on where the planets were located when you were born. This information is often presented as a small graph next to the chart wheel. A quick look at that information will help you identify energies that are not naturally available to you, or you may have an abundance of one type of elemental energy and need to balance it out.

For example, if you have five planets in the earth element, three in water, and one each in fire and air, then you are likely to find working with stones associated with fire and/or air to be stimulating and strengthening to your energy body. With the majority of your planets being in earth, you won't have the same need for supplemental earth energies, so those stones are less likely to be attractive to you.

Working the Magic

For many of us, choosing a stone is the easy part, but it is the "putting that stone to work" thing that gets us in trouble. Our crystal allies aren't just pretty things; they are partners waiting to rise to the occasion to help us. Once you have chosen an ally to work with, it is really important that you make an effort to do so regularly. It isn't the stone itself that does the magic or the heavy lifting, but rather the stone gives us the extra resources we need to do those things for ourselves. This means that we need to be regularly exposed to the stone for it to have any lasting value. Putting it on your mantel and walking away or putting it behind glass and appreciating it from afar will only keep you from truly accessing its potential power.

In addition to regular exposure to a stone, you might want to consider programming it to further assist you in your work. Not all stones need to be programmed, but programming a stone does allow for a more focused approach to working with its energy. If you have a specific self-improvement goal in mind, programming is the way to go.

To program a stone for self-improvement, first cleanse it of any non-native energies. My preferred methods include sound bathing, which is performed by exposing a stone to a single tone for thirty seconds or more, and cleansing by moonlight, which is performed by placing your stone under moonlight overnight. Next, create a set of instructions or a single instruction for the stone, such as "assist me in getting new clients, help me find ways to better budget my money, and help me see opportunities for side jobs," or simply "assist me in finding a healthy relationship."

Visualize that thought as a seed of light in your mind, and spend a few moments fully conceptualizing the stone's fruitful work. See the energy around the stone's instructions shift or manifest, and think about what it will feel like for you emotionally once those things have happened. Take a few deep breaths and then send that seed of light into the stone.

Once the seed of light is inside the stone, visualize it expanding to fill the stone completely with your instructions. Perform this as often

In addition to regular exposure to a stone, you might want to consider programming it to further assist you in your work. Not all stones need to be programmed, but programming a stone does allow for a more focused approach to working with its energy.

as needed to give the working more strength or whenever you need to update the instructions.

You can expand this process by programming multiple stones and connecting them through a crystal grid. Grids generally work with sacred geometry, which helps the crystalline energies express themselves on multiple levels; in other words, grids aid in the "as above, so below" principle. By working with crystal grids, we can exponentially increase our impact in all worlds, another critical act for most effective energy workers.

Maintaining the Magic

The rest is all care and feeding. If you have stones that you frequently carry with you or wear, be sure to regularly cleanse and empower them. As you move with them throughout the day, they are absorbing just as much energy (positive or negative) as you are, and the deeper your bond with them grows, the more apparent this will become. By regularly cleansing them to keep them vibrating with their own natural frequency, you will ensure that no unintentional programming is done to your stones.

Additionally, I recommend "feeding" your stone's energy on a regular basis. By doing so, you not only are making time to energetically connect to your own working but are also able to pull from other sources of energy to propel your working. For example, during a full moon, you should consider setting your stone out to absorb the light. This will empower your crystal so it can do a more effective job at empowering you. The same goes for sunlight, though this is usually recommended only for clear or translucent stones. The color of any stone, especially those that are crystals, can bleach in direct sunlight, fading the rich tones it developed while incubating.

Hold your stone often and talk to it as if you were talking to a person. It likely won't talk back, but it could very well communicate with you in meditation or dreams. You may feel silly when you do this, but you will get over it as your stone starts to respond by bringing you more opportunities, deeper wisdom, and clearer messages.

Just as you would do with any friend, make time for your crystal ally, recognize it, and honor it, and when you have reached a goal it helped you with, give it offerings of fresh psychic energy in the form of one of those seeds of light.

Stones not only provide us with the energies we need to thrive but also help us produce the insights necessary for a rewarding life. Whether you know what it is that you are looking for or need a little help figuring it out, the mineral kingdom is full of allies who are here to help.

Devin Hunter (San Francisco Bay Area) is a bestselling author who holds initiations in multiple spiritual, occult, and esoteric traditions and is the founder of his own tradition, Sacred Fires, and cofounder of its offshoot community, Black Rose Witchcraft. His podcast, The Modern Witch, has helped thousands of people from all over the world empower themselves and discover their psychic and magical abilities. Devin is the co-owner of the Mystic Dream, a metaphysical store in Walnut Creek, CA, where he offers professional services as a medium and occultist.

Illustrator: Tim Foley

Garden Guardians: Protection at the Door

Monica Crosson

My garden is a place of respite during uncertain times. Along the garden path, the very air vibrates with the drone of bees and the beat of hummingbird wings as they fight for the sweet nectar of honeysuckle. Evenings belong to the spirits of nature that ride upon the breeze on silky threads of moonlight, and I wonder, as twilight settles in shades of indigo, if they are aware of the anxiety and uncertainty that permeates our mundane world. Then I feel the breath of wind on my face, reminding me that they are aware, and everything will be okay.

It is the garden that many of us turn to in times of uncertainty. Working the soil can reduce levels of the stress hormone cortisol. It distracts the mind from the causes of stress and provides it with something to focus on, and gives us a sense of control. So whether you have enough time and land to create a lavish garden or just place a few planted pots on a back porch or balcony, I encourage you to get your witchy hands dirty—it's good for your soul.

Since home is our sanctuary, let's talk about the wonderful array of protective plants that can provide a magickal barrier during uncertain times. Here are three of my favorite protective plants, along with a list of common herbs that are protective powerhouses.

Rue (*Ruta graveolens*)

I wonder how a person could possibly "rue the day" they came across the blue-green lacy foliage and bright-yellow flowers of rue? This famous line from Shakespeare's *Macbeth*, meaning to regret that something has happened, was attributed to rue for its strong scent, which arises from an irritating sap that can cause skin irritation for those who are sensitive. Although for many people this is reason enough not to grow this lovely herb, these are the same reasons why I believe rue makes a wonderfully strong plant ally for magickal workings.

In the garden, rue is a protective plant that will stand guard and keep negativity at bay. It makes a nice low shrub that grows approximately two feet tall and also works as a repellent to dogs and cats, as most pets do not like the smell of rue. In fact, it was thought that rue's potent aromatic scent gave it the ability to prevent the spreading of disease by repelling insects, fleas, and rodents that carried the plague. This is demonstrated in a tale that survives to this day of four thieves who used the power of rue (and other healing herbs) as a preventative during one such deadly epidemic. Here is a modern version of the recipe.

Four Thieves Vinegar

- 16 ounces apple cider vinegar

- Cloves from one bulb of garlic (for its antibacterial and antiviral properties)

- 2 tablespoons each of the following four herbs (one herb for each thief):

  * Rue (anti-inflammatory, antispasmodic)

  * Thyme (antimicrobial, antibacterial)

  * Sage (antibacterial, antioxidant)

  * Rosemary (antibacterial, antioxidant)

Place the mixture in a container and let sit in a cool, dark place for 2–4 weeks. Strain into a clean jar, making sure to express all the liquid.

Traditionally, this vinegar was used much as hand sanitizer is used today, by rubbing it on the hands when approaching someone who was ill. Modern uses of four thieves vinegar include the following:

Immune-boosting tonic: Take several teaspoons per day to prevent colds or flu.

Cleanser: Use to sterilize kitchen and bathroom counters.

Astringent: Dilute with water and use as a skin astringent.

Salad dressing/marinade: Great used in vinaigrette and marinade recipes.

Insect repellent: Dilute 2 parts vinegar with ½ part water and add to a spray bottle for a safe, organic bug spray.

In magick: Use to repel negativity or a toxic person and in spells for protection and healing.

Mullein (*Verbascum* spp.)

Mullein stands guard much like the warrior crone it represents, with wisdom, strength, and grace. It is an ally that isn't picky about where it plants its roots and grows easily in the poorest of soils. In fact, mullein has probably caught your eye when driving along country roads, for this tall biennial beauty, which can reach up to eight feet, with densely haired leaves and tiny bright yellow flowers, is at home near roadside ditches. Medicinally, mullein is used for soothing coughs, colds, and asthma and as a poultice for sore muscles, sprains, and joint pain. Magickally, it is an herb of protection from malevolent magick and is said to drive away evil spirits.

Hag Tapers for the Modern Witch

As the light fades and a crisp breeze ushers in autumn, mullein forms long, heavy seed heads and stalks that stiffen, making it the perfect plant to use for torches. It is said that country folk dipped the seed heads in melted lard and used the makeshift torch as a way to light darkened paths that wound through forests and guarded witches' rites. I have made hag tapers for Samhain sabbats and find that when they do burn steady, they are lovely and mystical and harken back to a time when witches gathered under starry skies in the dead of night. But they can catch fire quickly, and you could be left with a mess of hot wax dripping on your hand as you run quickly to toss it into your sabbat fire before you and your surroundings go up in flames.

For those of you who would like to try using hag tapers as a protective element in your practice but need something a little safer than what I just described, here is a great way to mix a little Old World witchery into your modern Craft. This version of a hag taper is basically a fire-starter. These tapers work great to kindle your sacred flame and are perfect for Samhain, with the addition of rosemary, sage, and calendula. Of course, you can roll them in the dried herbs of your choosing. You will need:

- 1–2 dried stalks of mullein with seed head attached
- Several teaspoons each of dried rosemary, sage, and calendula (or other dried herbs of your choosing)
- 1 sheet baking parchment paper
- ½ pound beeswax, melted (You may need to adjust the amount depending on the size and number of tapers you make.)
- Tongs

Cut the mullein stalks into 3-to-6-inch lengths. Mix the dried herbs and spread them out on the parchment paper. Use tongs to completely coat the stalks in the melted beeswax and roll them in the herbal mixture. Let dry overnight. They are ready now to spark your sabbat fire by placing them in a large cauldron or firepit with kindling.

Holly (*Ilex* spp.)

During the darkest months of the year, as most of nature lies dormant under a blanket of snow, we are drawn inward to face those things that challenge us the most, and some of us struggle with the melancholy that the dreariness of winter can trigger. But outside, there is a sign that the light will return and that life persists: a small evergreen tree with leathery, lobed leaves, which can reach thirty feet in height and thrives in the darkest corners of the garden. The holly tree is one of the great guardians of nature. Brought into homes at Yule, it protects the occupants from malevolent energy and provides respite to nature spirits. Its ever-present green leaves reflect the light and its bright red berries contradict the rules of nature, making this plant a magickal one indeed.

A tea can be made from the leaves of holly to relieve the effects of bronchitis and as a fever reducer. The berries are toxic to humans and should not be consumed, although they are an important food source for birds.

Holly's white wood burns hot, which makes it a wonderful kindling for a midwinter balefire. It makes a beautiful wand, and a holly wreath hung on the door during midwinter is an attractive way to take advantage of its protective properties. But my favorite way to utilize holly's energy is by making holly water.

> **Holly's white wood burns hot, which makes it a wonderful kindling for a midwinter balefire. It makes a beautiful wand.**

HOLLY WATER

As I gather holly for midwinter decoration, I take a few sprigs to add to a bowl of water and charge under December's Long Nights Moon. You can use the water to cleanse the negative energy from magickal tools or sprinkle it around the home with a sprig of fir as an aspergillum to chase away bad vibes. I typically do this when the winter doldrums set in, after which I light a few candles and practice a little self-care.

To make holly water, you will need:

- A couple sprigs of freshly clipped holly (Remember to be reverent of the tree.)

- A large bowl of water

On the night of the December full moon, place the sprigs of holly in the bowl of water and set in a window to charge under the full moon's light.

Standing Guard

Here are some more protective plants for your home or garden.

Angelica: This lovely plant keeps nasty spirits at bay. Keep a piece of angelica root in a pouch for personal protection.

Cactus: This plant is the ultimate ward! If you can't grow cactus outdoors, have a few in your windowsills. Use the spines in witch bottles or protective amulets.

Garden sage: Use garden sage in place of traditional white sage in smudge bundles and incense mixes to clear negativity.

Honeysuckle: Plant this prolific climber near your front door to keep illness and bad vibes away and to attract luck.

Juniper: This beautiful tree is strongly protective and can be planted to keep negative energy from harming your home; it negates hexes.

Ferns: Ferns are a wonderful addition to any garden and a fairy favorite. Plant them to protect from curses: sprinkle them around the property for invisibility.

Mugwort: Because of its association with divination and honing psychic abilities, this lovely herb is great for warding off psychic attacks.

Rosemary: A powerful protector and purifier when burned as incense, rosemary grows well in pots on a sunny porch or balcony.

CIRCLE OF LIGHT BATH SALTS

Don't let the psychic vampires get you down! These bath salts made with protective dried herbs and essential oils are just the thing to cleanse away those bad vibes and make you feel like you're floating in a circle of light. You will need:

- 4 cups Epsom salt
- ½ cup baking soda
- 1 cup melted coconut oil
- ½ cup dried mugwort
- ¼ cup dried sage
- 20 drops rosemary oil
- 10 drops lavender oil

Mix all of the ingredients by hand in a bowl while repeating the following:

Protect,
Purify,
Sanctify me.

Store in a glass jar and sprinkle one cup into your bath.

Magickal Plants for Highly Sensitive People

I am a highly sensitive person (HSP) who is easily overwhelmed by the energy of others. When in a crowded room, I feel like a porch light that draws so many moths that my light becomes smothered and I ultimately shut down. Not only do I take in the light and lovely energies of warm and caring individuals, but I also absorb negative energies such as anger, mistrust and pain, which feed my own insecurities and make me run back to my enchanted forest as fast as I can.

Highly sensitive person disorder is a term used for people with sensory processing sensitivity. It is found in 4 to 5 percent of the population and is identified as an increased sensitivity of the central nervous system and a deeper cognitive processing of physical, social, and emotional stimuli. In other words, people with this disorder are more aware of the subtle energies at play and process information deeply. We experience the world differently, and that's why (I believe) so many of us attune so well to the natural world.

Here is a list of protective herbs especially for highly sensitive people to keep in pots or plant close to entrances of the home:

Agrimony: Healing and restoration

Birch: Psychic protection

Calendula: Repairs the aura and provides energetic protection

Cedar: Healing and protective

Chamomile: Relaxes energy and allows you to become more receptive

Comfrey: Healing and restoration

Fennel: Healing and focus; wards off negativity

Hibiscus: Acceptance of self

Lavender: Healing and calming

Lemon balm: Restoration and harmony

Valerian: Transmutes negativity

Shielding Oil

One way I like to help protect myself is by applying a few drops of shielding oil to my pulse points and temple before going into highly charged situations. The shielding properties of cinnamon and cedar combined with the uplifting scent of orange make this oil a lifesaver for HSPs. (Note: Cinnamon oil can be an irritant for some people.) You will need:

- ⅓ ounce carrier oil (Grapeseed and fractionated coconut oil are great choices.)

- 5 drops cinnamon oil

- 3 drops cedar oil

- 2 drops orange oil

- Glass roll vial

Mix the ingredients together and add to the vial. Shake and allow to sit overnight before use.

RESTORATION TEA

When I return home after being in a charged situation, there is nothing that helps me reset like a good cup of restoration tea.

- 2 parts calendula

- 1 part chamomile

- ½ part lemon balm

These three restorative herbs blend nicely for a relaxing brew. Place in a tea ball and steep in a mug of hot water for at least five minutes. Enjoy!

Monica Crosson (*Concrete, WA*) *has been a practicing witch and educator for over thirty years and is a member of Evergreen Coven. She is the author of* The Magickal Family *and* Wild Magical Soul *and is a regular contributor to the Llewellyn annuals as well as magazines such as* Enchanted Living *and* Witchology.

Illustrator: Rik Olson

The Well-Groomed Witch: Magical Self-Care for the Discerning Practitioner

Storm Faerywolf

Grooming is an essential part of human socialization and care. Bathing. Cutting hair. Shaving. Trimming nails. Brushing teeth. We are taught at an early age how to practice basic care and hygiene for our physical body, but rarely are we also taught the same for our spiritual nature. Every act that we might consider to be mundane has the potential to be a vessel for our magical intention. There is the possibility for magic in everything we do, right down to our basic self-care routines.

I'd wager that most people generally want to look their best. Perhaps it's to make a good impression and ace that job interview. It might be to catch the attention of a special someone in the hopes of igniting something more. But it doesn't have to be about anyone else. Maybe it's simply because when you look your best, you feel your best. And when you feel your best, you project positive energy, which in turn impacts and informs your actions in the world. When you feel good, you are more likely to do well.

When you look your best, you feel your best. And when you feel your best, you project positive energy, which in turn impacts and informs your actions in the world. When you feel good, you are more likely to do well.

Whatever the underlying reasons, there is nothing wrong with taking pride in one's appearance. It's a very personal thing, and because it's so personal, there is also the potential to generate a lot of magical power if we commit to establishing some level of discipline.

If your initial reaction to the above statement was one of dread, I have some good news for you: In no way does establishing a type of magical discipline need to be difficult or boring. There is an easy way to do it that will not require you to make sweeping changes to your current lifestyle. Instead, you can make small augmentations to your current routine simply by changing your relationship to it and adding a couple simple, easy observances. In other words, you can take your basic grooming routine and inject it with a healthy dose of magic.

Anything we do repetitively can be considered a ritual, such as brushing our teeth and combing our hair. These are basic rituals that we learn early on, and because we have performed them so many times over the years, they have taken on a momentum. Because these activities have been largely unconscious, they lack the magical and spiritual cohesion that we usually attempt to form when we engage in our "normal" (i.e., consciously or ritually focused) magical activities. Left as such, they are something akin to an empty container, just waiting to be filled with the magic of our Craft.

This type of witchcraft draws in part from our primal self, that deep source of internal power. The ecstatic practices of witchcraft give us access to these deeper states of awareness and power, so we may then use these practices to enliven those that are normally "lifeless."

The following practices can be done with no additional tools or ingredients other than what you would normally use. You may, of course, expand these with the addition of certain herbs, candles, oils, etc., and where there are good suggestions for those, I have added as much to the text below. The only thing that is required is a willingness to engage in the otherwise "boring" daily chores of taking care of your body with a renewed sense of spiritual and magical focus and maybe the memorization (or creation) of some simple cantrips designed to focus your magical attention.

A Modern Khernips (Hand Washing Rite)

Many readers might be familiar with the Hellenic practice of *khernips*, which is a ritual cleansing involving the washing of the hands and sometimes the face. It is traditional to combine fresh and sea waters into a bowl, then burn a leaf or twig and toss the smoldering substance into the water, often with the exclamation "Xerniptosai!" ("Zer-nip-TOS-aye-ee"), which means "be purified!" This is a very beautiful and potent ritual and one that my own coven has adapted and observed at the beginning of our meetings for as far back as I can remember. But as simple as this is, it isn't something that you could necessarily do on the go. Here's a quick exercise inspired by the traditional version that can be done anywhere you have access to a sink and running water, whether you're at home, on vacation, or even in a gas station restroom!

Before you place your hands under the water, use your imagination to tap into the elements of fire and earth, and imagine them being directed into the faucet and pipes in order to infuse the water with their essence. Say (or think strongly to yourself):

Xerniptosai!

As you wash your hands, recite (or think) the following while imagining yourself becoming light and purified:

Lustral waters, here I conjure.
Wash away impurities.

Facing the Day (Face Washing Rite)

Splashing cold water on the face is a good way to help wake us up after a long night's sleep, as well as to assist us in returning to our body after heavy astral and trance work. This rite is designed to be done each morning, but you can adapt it to serve you best.

Begin by performing the modern khernips rite. Leaning over your sink, fill your hands with cold water. Wash your face as normal, perhaps using your preferred cleanser or soap. Rinse by quickly splashing your face. Repeat as needed while saying:

Water, cleanse away the night;
Alert, alive, refreshed, renewed.

Use the towel to gently pat your face dry, feeling yourself become focused in the present moment and alert to your surroundings. Look at yourself in the mirror as you conjure up a sense of confidence.

Exaltation of the Body (Body Washing Rite)

This exercise allows us to have a meditative and magical experience while we are taking a "normal" shower or bath. You may wish to use soaps containing herbal elements that are magically aligned with your personal intentions, such as peppermint to sharpen the mind, rose for love and compassion, or lavender for balance and harmony. But you don't need anything fancy to engage in this form of magical bathing; just your normal soap and maybe a cloth or puff will do. Feel free to adapt this rite to better suit your needs.

Before you even get in the water, while turning on the faucet, focus your intention on the water element and its qualities: cleansing, the subconscious, transformation. Then say:

I *call to water to cleanse my body.*
I *call to water to cleanse my soul.*
I *call to water to cleanse my spirit.*
I *call to water to cleanse my mind.*

Now in the bath or shower, and using your preferred soap, lather up and focus on certain key areas of the body, reciting or otherwise consciously focusing on the basic intention behind each line of the following incantation. Imagine these statements as being true in a poetic-magical sense. As you focus your washing and your intention on each area of your body, use your creativity and passion to help empower your visualizations and affirmations.

My crown is bright and worn with pride.
My eldritch eye is sharp and keen.
My ears hear whispers on the wind.
My voice commands the worlds unseen.
My heart aflame engulfs the world.
My arms embrace with strength and poise.

My center, strong as oaken wood.
My sex, the source of life and joy.
My roots are stable in the land.
My legs are bolstered, strong I stand.
My feet are firm upon my path,
To keep me clear of harm or wrath.
My body clean, my spirit clear,
My mind and soul shall persevere.

Rinse and towel dry, feeling yourself purified and ready to engage in deep magical work…or maybe just a trip to the grocery store.

The Power of Hair and Nails: Trimming, Shaving, Styling, and Plucking

We as a species spend a lot of time and energy on our hair and nails. From styling to the removal of unwanted hair to the trimming and lacquering of our nails, the care and styling of hair and nails is a lucrative industry.

The shaving, trimming, and styling of the hair and nails is one of the pieces of forbidden knowledge said to have been bestowed on humankind by the Watchers, fallen angels who, according to folklore, interbred with humans and were responsible for teaching certain arts such as magic, warfare, and, yes, cosmetics. So, technically, grooming and taking care of your appearance is witchcraft.

Let's take that magic that we're already performing and do something more with it. When shaving and/or trimming your hair, beard, or nails (or applying makeup or nail polish, using moisturizers, etc.), recite the following or a similar incantation:

Sculpted is my image here,
To others, how I shall appear:

See me strong and see me proud.
See me kind and see me wise.
See me happy and see me bright.
[...]

You can make this list as long or short as you need, though shorter affirmations tend to work best, as they allow us more focus. If you can, repeat this incantation like a chant until you move into a trance. When you are done, end with these words:

The me I choose, the me you see.

Your Magic Mouth (Teeth-Brushing Rite)

Taking care of our teeth and gums is an essential part of our overall self-care. Certain ailments such as heart disease and pneumonia can actually start as a result of poor dental hygiene, making dental care much more important than just to maintain a pretty smile (though who doesn't want that?). Even if our teeth are already damaged, we must do whatever we can to keep our mouth clean to prevent further disease, as well as to help direct however else we might be using our mouth, namely, how we direct our speech.

The words we speak are the carriers of vibration and intention. Each time we make an affirmation, it is like a tiny invocation, moving energy in a given direction and summoning specific energies into our lives. If we spend a lot of time making positive affirmations, we are more likely to attract positive energies. The same is true of negative affirmations and energies.

The American Dental Association recommends that everyone brush their teeth with a soft bristle brush for two minutes. Harder bristles can actually damage the enamel on your teeth, and soft bristles are better able to get underneath the gumline, which helps prevent infection.

Using your usual toothpaste, brush your teeth normally while mentally reciting the following for the recommended duration of two minutes. (I recommend setting a timer, perhaps on your phone.)

My words are clear.
My words precise.
My words are true.
My words are kind.

Depending on what kind of toothpaste you use, you may be able to employ certain plant spirits to assist you with more specific intentions, such as mint for cooling the mind and tongue or cinnamon for adding fire and passion.

. . . .

Everything we do to take care of ourselves has an inner counterpart. We are not just augmenting our outer self in a vain attempt to hide our true inner self; we are allowing our inner beauty to come out and take part in our lives on all levels. Let every act of basic self-care be a magical affirmation of your continued health, success, beauty, and power as you live and grow. Look into that mirror with pride and hear the words of the Faery Blue God: "Behold how beautiful you are!"

Storm Faerywolf *is a professional warlock. Drawn to the Craft at an early age, he went on to be trained and initiated into various streams of witchcraft, most notably the Faery tradition, where he holds the Black Wand of a Master. He is the founder of BlueRose, a school and lineage of the Faery tradition, and is one of the founding teachers of Black Rose, an online school and style of practical folkloric witchcraft. He is a regular contributor to* Modern Witch *and a columnist for* The Wild Hunt. *He is the author of several books, including* Betwixt & Between: Forbidden Mysteries of Faery Witchcraft *and* The Stars Within the Earth. *Visit Faerywolf.com for more.*

Illustrator: Bri Hermanson

Self-Care as Devotion to the Divine

Mat Auryn

As witches, most of us work with spirits and deities in one form or another, and are eager to please them and devote time to them.

Growing up, my views of service and devotion were always selfless. This began to shift after an experience at the Feast of Hekate, an unofficial sabbat celebrated by many modern witches as the ninth holiday on the wheel of the year. It honors Hekate as the goddess of storms in the month of August and petitions her to keep the storms (both literal and metaphorical) at bay in our lives. At the peak of this ritual, three priestesses put on a

veil of either black, red, or white and aspect one of Hekate's triple forms. Aspecting is when a priest or priestess ritually calls upon a deity or spirit to overshadow or overlight them for oracular communication, similar in some ways yet different from the idea of channeling or ritual possession and more akin to the Drawing Down the Moon ritual in Wicca. The attendants circle the priestesses, chanting and singing and keeping the energy high. One by one, each attendee gets the opportunity to sit with Hekate to ask her a question via her priestess oracles.

When it was my time to ask the oracle a question, I went and sat with the veiled priestess. I had a burning question inside of me, one of care for my community. "How can I help and serve my community spiritually?" I asked.

She responded with another question: "How are you helping and serving yourself? Before you can help and serve others, you must learn how to help and serve yourself first. The two are a reflection of each other." These words have stuck with me for many years ever since.

While there's definite truth to this simple oracular statement, I've also come to see self-service and self-care in a different light—that of serving the self as a reflection of serving the divine.

When it comes to working with our deities, witches often give physical and non-physical offerings. Physical offerings can be food, drink, incense, or other objects that the spirit finds favorable. We give non-physical offerings in the form of time, energy, song, prayer, dance, chant, and

Physical offerings can be food, drink, incense, or other objects that the spirit finds favorable. We give non-physical offerings in the form of time, energy, song, prayer, dance, chant, and sometimes worship.

sometimes worship. Offerings feed, nourish, and please the spirit or divinity. Our desire to give to others from a place of selflessness is a strongly ingrained spiritual concept in Western religion and spirituality, but it's not necessarily the correct approach for a witch.

Thou Art God/dess

In most witchcraft traditions, there is an emphasis on being either a spark of divinity or a child of divinity. Many traditions place a strong emphasis on realizing and actualizing our own inherent divinity, or, through effort, elevating into the role of merging back with the divine through apotheosis within one or (more likely) many lifetimes. This is an idea inherent in the Chaldean Oracles, a poem outlining the nature of reality and divinity that was written during the second century CE by either Julian the Theurgist or his father, Julian the Chaldean, while in a trance state. The actual text of the Chaldean Oracles has been lost aside from fragments, and most of what we know about it are from the writings of Neoplatonists quoting and discussing it.

Within the Chaldean Oracles, the name of the Goddess is Hekate, who is seen as the Cosmic Soul of the three realms of the Upper World, Lower World, and Middle World. She is the source from which all souls emerge and to which they will return in the cycle of reincarnation until she can guide us to a reunion with that Unknowable Supreme Spirit and step off the cycle of rebirth. This is why Hekate is often referred to by the epithet *Soteira*, meaning "Savior."

As such, the notion suggests that not only do we come from the divine, but our three souls of mind, body, and spirit are inherently divine in and of themselves. Therefore, it is only logical to conclude that neglecting ourselves is neglecting the most immediate relationship with divinity to which we have access: our indwelling divinity. As empowered witches, we must be mindful of how we offer our time, energy, actions, and choices to feed, nourish, please, and in turn strengthen ourselves and our power.

A lack of self-care can lead to burnout. When we are burned out, we may have more difficulty devoting time and energy to our gods and each other. In turn, we offer less of ourselves. By viewing ourselves as part of an interconnected web of divinity that includes others and ourselves, we can approach devotion in a balanced and healthy manner. Maintaining personal balance means we should not view self-care as a form of escapism, laziness, or hedonism. At the same time, we should strive to ensure we are not in a position of denying the self. If we view self-care as selfish and don't allow ourselves to rest or have pleasure, we are susceptible to dishonoring and exhausting the self.

The simplest way to transform self-care into self-devotion is through reframing how we approach mundane acts of self-care. Through a simple shift of mindfulness, we can magickally and spiritually empower these acts of self-service.

Food and Drink as Offerings to the Self

By taking a mindful moment to bless our food and drink, we can energetically offer it to ourselves. Through maintaining a healthy diet, we offer ourselves energy, strength, and nourishment. By indulging in food and drink that is less than healthy, we bring enjoyment and pleasure to ourselves. A simple form of blessing food as an offering can be as simple as taking a moment before eating and drinking to envision the food or drink glowing with a white light and stating, "I bless this offering to the divine within me so that it may nourish, strengthen, energize, and heal me on all levels." Likewise, we might say, "I bless this offering to the divine within me so that it may bring pleasure, enjoyment, and happiness to me on all levels."

Communion with the Self

Performing inner work is one of the most powerful ways we can honor ourselves for the purposes of self-care. By spending time in reflection, we can commune with ourselves. By understanding ourselves, processing our experiences, and striving to grow as individuals, we strengthen our ability to understand and commune with others and the divine.

Regular journaling is one of the most powerful ways you can process and grow as a person. Aside from the cathartic element of journaling, you may surprise yourself with what comes out through the act of honestly expressing your thoughts and feelings. Journaling can help us understand who we truly are, recognize and honor our personal accomplishments and strengths, and bring awareness to the parts of ourselves that we may need to work on.

Journaling can help us understand who we truly are, recognize and honor our personal accomplishments and strengths, and bring awareness to the parts of ourselves that we may need to work on.

Likewise, through meditative practices, we can learn how our mental processes work by simply observing what comes up during meditation. By framing meditation as a time to rest and a chance to strengthen our psychic and intuitive abilities, we can find enjoyment in it instead of viewing it as another chore on our spiritual to-do list. In turn, strengthening these abilities allows us to have a stronger connection with our deities and spirits through becoming more receptive and perceptive to their presence and communication in our lives.

Adorning the Shrine of Self

As witches, we spend a lot of time and energy decorating and maintaining our altars and shrines as a form of respect, ensuring that everything is clean and tidy. We should reflect upon whether we are giving our own dwelling spaces and our body (sometimes referred to as the soul's temple) the same amount of attention and respect by ensuring that we are grooming, maintaining, and beautifying ourselves and our living spaces. This act of self-devotion is also an act of devotion to the divine.

With mindful intention, self-care can be a powerful act of devotion to everything beyond ourselves and give us a frame of reference for how to honor and care for others.

Mat Auryn (Bay Area) *is a witch, professional psychic, and occult teacher. He is the international bestselling author of* Psychic Witch: A Metaphysical Guide to Meditation, Magick & Manifestation. *He is a high priest in the Sacred Fires Tradition of Witchcraft. As a psychic witch, Mat has had the honor and privilege of studying under some of the most prominent witchcraft teachers and elders. He runs the blog* For Puck's Sake *on Patheos Pagan, is a content creator for* Modern Witch, *and writes a column called* Extra-Sensory Witchcraft *for* Witches & Pagans *magazine as well as a column for* Horns *magazine. Mat has been featured in various magazines, radio shows, podcasts, books, anthologies, and periodicals. To find out more about him and his work, visit www.MatAuryn.com.*

Illustrator: M. Kathryn Thompson

Witchy Living

DAY-BY-DAY WITCHCRAFT

The (Mostly) Self-Sufficient Witch: Make Your Own Tools & Supplies

Autumn Damiana

The events of 2020 showed me that it is more important than ever, or at least more convenient, to be as self-sufficient as a Witch can be. This has been a trying time, but it has also taught me that I've always had the resources I need for my rituals and spells. Magic is everywhere. We tend to think that the more rare or exotic something is, the more magical it must be, but this is not true. Everything in the natural world has energy in it that can be tapped, and the more familiar something is, the more likely it will have personal power and meaning.

Maybe I don't have fancy tools or supplies to work with, but aside from crystals and essential oils, I can find just about anything I need (or a good substitution) at hand, often from my own house or yard. This way, I can save my money for a few nice, quality items. And if I buy them from the magical community, I'm helping to support my witchy brothers and sisters in the process.

Two of the projects listed below will require a slow cooker, so if you don't have one, borrow it or find one secondhand. Find out more about magical correspondences in the suggested reading list at the end.

Instant Altar Tools

Most Witches work with at least one or two altar tools, usually an athame or a wand for directing energy. Here are some altar tool arrangements that make use of common objects that are free, cheap, and inconspicuous, to protect your privacy. These tool "kits" are listed in this order: air/athame, fire/wand, water/chalice, and earth/pentacle.

- **Basic altar:** pocket or Swiss Army knife, chopstick or twig, shot glass or small cup, coin or flat round stone

- **Kitchen Witch:** favorite kitchen knife, wooden spoon, wine glass or water goblet, special plate or platter

- **Garden Witch:** spade, wood or metal plant spike, small sealed glazed pot, terracotta saucer

- **Book Witch:** letter opener, special pencil or pen, mug or teacup, coaster

You can mix and match these tools or leave some out altogether. The truth is that you don't need tools to work magic, but most Witches find it much easier to concentrate on their workings and direct energy using these magical "props." Use objects made from natural materials, such as stone, paper, metal, glass, wood, and ceramic, and make sure to cleanse and consecrate your tools before using them. Here is a simple ritual you can use.

Ritual to Cleanse and Consecrate Tools

Invest in a nice chunky piece of selenite. This crystal has wonderful purifying properties and doesn't need to be cleared very often. Move the crystal over your tools, and visualize negative vibes being sucked up like a vacuum cleaner by the crystal. Set it aside, then lay your dominant hand on the tools and raise your receptive hand high, palm up. Speak this elemental charm:

Land and sea, sun and sky,
Powers low and powers high,
Mingle where my spirit lives,
And by my hand your blessings give.

Visualize the power of the elements filling your body. Earth and water are drawn up from the ground through your legs, and fire and air are drawn down into your arm. They meet at your heart and mix with your spirit. This pure energy then flows out through your dominant hand and into your tools. They are now dedicated and ready for use. You can repeat this ritual on anything you wish to consecrate. And when your selenite feels "dirty" or "overworked," lay it on the ground outside or in the moonlight (or both) overnight to cleanse it. (Do NOT use water or salt.) Or use the following purification method.

Purification Method Using Sound

If you have a crystal glass, bowl, or vase, you can use it for sound healing. Tap it with different objects to make it ring: use a spoon or chopstick, flick it with your finger, or rub around the rim. Be creative and see what else produces an appealing tone. Add water to it to change the pitch. When you find a sound that resonates with you, hold the selenite just above the vessel when you play it to cleanse the crystal. You can also cleanse any other crystal or object, and you can even use this method to clear a room!

Beyond Kitchen Witchery

I have always had a "trash to treasure" philosophy in that I try to use materials that are byproducts of other things I own or purchase. For example, I save the metal lids from frozen juice cans to use as wax catchers under my tea and votive candles. The best part is that the lid is something useful that I have as the result of buying the juice, which I was going to get anyway.

Kitchen witchery is immensely popular, and I know most Witches are pretty savvy these days when it comes to using kitchen staples, like how to substitute ordinary cooking herbs and spices in magical recipes. I have taken things further and found applications for items beyond the kitchen that would typically end up in the garbage or recycling bin. Here are some ideas.

- I'll say it again: Hang on to all your stale or expired dried herbs and spices, because their magical correspondences remain the same and they can still be included in your workings.

- Don't stop there! If you can't use an item for food and it won't mold, rot, or go rancid, consider keeping it for spells and rituals. This includes stale nuts, crystallized sugar, old coffee beans, and grains (oats, beans, popcorn, rice, etc.) that are past their prime.

- Burn a cinnamon stick and use the smoke to banish negativity, like you would with palo santo.

- Use an egg carton to hold and organize crystals. You can write inside or on top of the carton what the crystal is charged with, the date you cleansed it, how you cleansed it, etc. Recycle the container and start again as needed.

- Make a pillow box with a toilet paper roll. This is a simple substitution for a spell box or even a bag or jar in a pinch. Just flatten the tube halfway with your hand, so it is oval instead of round, then fold the ends down like flaps.

- Forget buying expensive fiberfill. Use your dryer lint, spent dryer sheets, or old clothes cut into pieces to stuff poppets and small dream pillows.

- Save and wash eggshells. These can be pulverized with a mortar and pestle to make Cascarilla Powder, which is a potent hoodoo recipe for luck and protection.

- Make a "junk mail" Book of Shadows. Use only glossy photos, like from magazines, catalogs, and high-quality advertisements. Find elemental correspondences from chimney sweeping, fireplace, and barbecue ads (fire); pool, sprinkler, and water feature ads (water); window cleaning and filter/air purification or attic cleaning ads (air); and landscaping and house cleaning or organizing ads (earth). Also look for pictures of happy babies or children (fertility), happy couples (love), or attractive real estate ads (home magic). Pictures of gardens are good for the Green Witch, images of food work for kitchen witchery, and ads about security systems are perfect for protection magic. Also take a close look at the various catalogs you receive—they will likely represent your tastes and interests, which make them perfect to use in your Book of Shadows. Or use those images in spells or to make a vision board.

- If you cast a spell for yourself, it helps to add a bit of yourself to the mix. You can add a strand of hair, an eyelash, or some spit.

Also consider adding the clippings from a fingernail or toenail, some cream you shaved with, the cloth you used to take off your makeup, or even the tissue that you blotted your lipstick on or used to blow your nose. These are far less nasty than the blood or urine that some older spells require.

Nature's Gifts

As Witches, we are more in tune with the Earth than most people, and we know that it provides us with everything we need for our magical practice. Of course, this includes pretty, precious things like crystals and flowers, but what about nature's other gifts? Here are some often ignored but equally useful things that we can find in nature.

SPIDER WEBS

Spider silk has a tensile strength similar to that of steel. Use it in binding spells, especially to wrap around a scroll, poppet, candle, etc., that you have used to bind that person or thing from doing you harm. Use old webs (there's always one lurking somewhere) and don't evict a spider from its home!

ROCKS

All rocks can be used for multiple applications. Rocks embody the element of earth and can be employed in earth-related spells or used to symbolize this element on your altar. Any rock or stone from your yard can be charged with protective powers and placed at the four corners of your property, home, or room.

Here is another rock spell. Find a rock and hold it in your lap. Channel anything you want to be rid of into the rock. When you have filled the rock with all of your woes, toss it into a body of water. It will sink to the bottom, and the earth will absorb the negativity while the water will help to wash it away.

Dirt

Use very fine dark dirt or dust from your yard or surrounding area to make a magical ink. Mix the dirt with water until it forms a thick paste. Add herbs to charge it with intent. Then paint the dirt mixture onto white paper to make magical symbols or sigils. Let the mixture dry completely (it helps to put it out in the sun or in a warm oven), then brush off the dried mud remains.

Sand

Place sand in any container, and you can safely burn a charcoal tablet with loose incense on top. But you can also use sand in spells and rituals. Gather sand from the footprint of anyone you want to work a spell for, including yourself. You can also do this with mud.

Ash

Save the ash from incense, a fireplace/firepit, or even tobacco, and add it to salt to make a black salt that can be used for protection.

Weeds

We all hate weeds, but they have much to offer us. Consider the characteristics of a weed: strength, persistence, adaptation, and defiance, to name just a few. These are all very desirable attributes in spellcraft, so go ahead and use them. Get in touch with the plant spirit of the weed, or use your imagination.

Dead Bugs

You can use dead bugs to connect with the animal kingdom without harm, provided you don't kill the bugs yourself. Roll a bug tightly in a piece of tissue and wrap it with tape to make a kind of capsule. Avoid working with dangerous insects and pests, since they carry negative associations. You can use the following:

- Ants for strength

- Bees for cooperation

- Beetles for protection

- Butterflies for change or transformation

- Crickets for love

- Dragonflies for magic and spirituality

- Ladybugs for luck

- Moths for secrecy and camouflage

- Spiders for creativity or to "catch" new opportunities

Infused Oils

You can't make essential oils without special equipment, but you can infuse an oil with a plant's magical properties to use for anointing yourself or your tools or for dressing a candle.

Materials needed:

- Whole herbs, spices, and other plant matter (Use only edible ones if you will be applying the oil to your skin!)

- Slow cooker

- Olive, almond, grapeseed, avocado, coconut, or other oil

- Colander or mesh strainer

- Cheesecloth or a piece of cotton (An old t-shirt works well.)

- Bowl

1. Pack your herbs and spices tightly in the slow cooker.

2. Pour in your oil of choice until it just covers the plants.

3. Cover and heat the oil on low for at least eight hours. The longer you can heat it, the better.

4. Turn off the slow cooker and let the mixture cool.

5. Line your colander or strainer with cheesecloth or cotton, and place it over a bowl.

6. Pour the herb oil into the strainer. Let this sit for a few hours to drain.

7. Gather up the cloth and squeeze the remaining oil out of it and into the bowl.

8. Throw away the cloth and bottle your infused oil. Any new or used glass bottle or jar will work as long as it is completely clean and dry. Store the oil in the fridge to keep it from going rancid.

Herbal Potion Spritz

I love to use this potion instead of incense to cleanse a space or an object. You can also make a spell potion by changing the ingredients you include in the spray bottle. You will need these materials:

- Whole fragrant herbs, flowers, or spices

- Small spray bottle

- Crystals (optional)—Amethyst and clear quartz are good all-purpose stones. Or use a plain old rock for "earthy" influences such as grounding and stability.

- Water

- Lavender-scented witch hazel

- Essential oils that pair well with lavender—Try rosemary or sage for purification, mint or basil for money and prosperity, rose for love, any evergreen for longevity, any citrus for happiness, cedar for protection, eucalyptus for health, etc.

1. Pick your plant material. Many things go well with lavender. Choose herbs and flowers and even spices such as cinnamon, cloves, or peppercorns.

2. Add your whole herbs, flowers, and spices (break up the spices for maximum scent) to the spray bottle.

3. Add any crystals if you are using them.

4. Fill the bottle half with water and half with the witch hazel.

5. Drop at least five drops of essential oils into the mix. (You can add more later if needed.)

6. Shake whenever you want to spritz your potion.

Recycled Candles

If there is a substantial amount of wax left over from a candle I have used, I save the wax and remelt it to make a new candle. This works best with candle wax that is all the same composition. For example, I do this with large jar candles that have burned down on one side but left a ton of wax on the other, or I save the ends of taper candles that were all part of a set. Melting unrelated candles together is not recommended, because the composition of different candles can be vastly different, and there is no guarantee that they will melt evenly or burn correctly.

Materials needed:

- Candle wax pieces

- Jar (See the suggestions on the next page.)

- Non-food-related knife (I use a dull paring knife set aside for crafts only.)

- Adhesive remover (optional)

- Wire-core candle wick (Get this at a craft store.)

- Hot glue gun or tape

- Pencil (optional)

- Slow cooker

1. Chop up your wax into small pieces. Wax cracks more easily than it cuts. If you jam your knife into the wax at different points, it will break apart on its own. If you are reusing the wax from a jar candle, get it out the same way, and repeat this process until pieces start to come free. Remove as much as you can, then freeze the jar. The remaining wax should pull away from the sides of the glass so you can remove it.

2. Pick your new jar. You can reuse any jar, such as a jar that once held a candle, or you can repurpose a food jar. Any jar with a metal lid that pops when you open it (such as for jelly/jam, pickles, condiments, etc.) can handle high temperatures, so they work well. You can also use actual canning jars or glazed ceramic containers. Mugs, teacups, and ramekins are all acceptable.

3. Prepare the jar. Remove all labels, using adhesive remover if necessary. Clean the jar thoroughly and let it air-dry.

4. Set your wick in place. Cut a piece of wick about ½ inch higher than the top of the jar. Using the hot glue gun, squeeze a glob of glue onto the end of the wick. Stick the glued end down into the center of the jar. Hold it in place until the glue sets, so your wick will stand up on its own. Or you can bend the end of the wick and use a piece of tape to secure it to the bottom of the jar,

using a pencil to press it into place. Make sure the wick is well adhered to the bottom and that the rest of the wick is centered where it stands up.

5. Add the wax pieces to the jar, and pack them tightly around the wick. Try to keep the wick centered.

6. Place the jar in a slow cooker on low, with water in it about ⅔ up the sides of the jar. Put the lid on the slow cooker and let it heat for several hours. Check it periodically to see if you need to add more water or if your wax has melted.

7. When all the wax has melted, you can add more wax to make the candle taller, and repeat the melting process. When you are finished, turn off the cooker and leave the candle in the water with the lid on to let it cool down to room temperature gradually. This will minimize pitting and cracking.

Suggested Reading

Blake, Deborah. *Witchcraft on a Shoestring*. Woodbury, MN: Llewellyn, 2010.

Cunningham, Scott. *Cunningham's Encyclopedia of Magical Herbs & Cunningham's Encyclopedia of Wicca in the Kitchen*. St. Paul: Llewellyn, 1999, 2004.

Rufus, Anneli, and Kristan Lawson. *The Scavengers' Manifesto*. New York: Penguin, 2009.

Autumn Damiana *is an author, artist, crafter, and amateur photographer. She is a solitary eclectic Cottage Witch who has been following her Pagan path for almost two decades and is a regular contributor to the Llewellyn annuals. Along with writing and making art, Autumn has a degree in early childhood education and is currently pursuing further studies. She lives with her husband and doggie familiar in the beautiful San Francisco Bay Area. Visit her online at autumndamiana.com.*

Illustrator: Tim Foley

Sunflowers: Allies in Magick

Jason Mankey

When I was a child, I spent my summers with my grandparents. Both of my grandparents did some gardening, but it was what my grandfather grew that has stayed with me over the years. Every summer he'd grow eight or so large sunflowers on a little patch of grass next to his garage. I would watch them sprout in May, and then marvel at just how tall they had gotten by late August. Some summers my brother and I would take pictures next to them every few weeks as they grew. By the end of summer, Grandpa's sunflowers would tower over us.

Sunflowers are like no other domestic plant crop we grow in our gardens. They can be amazingly tall, with some varieties reaching as high as sixteen feet. (The tallest sunflower ever grown was thirty feet high, but that's an anomaly.) They also grow quickly; the life span of a sunflower is only three to four months. Sunflowers are easy to cultivate. All that's required is a sunny spot and a medium-sized pot of dirt. If you lack a green thumb but want to experience the magick of growing something from a seedling to a mature plant, sunflowers are an excellent choice.

Sunflowers are native to North America and have been domesticated for over five thousand years. The original plant had multiple heads, and over the centuries was cultivated until it grew just one large head at the top of its stalk. Over the years, hundreds of varieties have been developed, in various sizes and colors. (Not all sunflowers are yellow.)

The sunflower is an extremely useful plant. We all know that its seeds can be eaten, but those seeds can also be turned into flour. The seeds also make an especially good cooking oil, one that contains various healthy unsaturated fats and has a high smoke point. The latter quality makes sunflower oil especially useful for frying things.

I value sunflowers for their beauty and usefulness, but as a Witch, they also make fine companions for my magickal endeavors. I use sunflowers and their seeds nearly all year long in my magickal work. I use the magick of sunflowers for protection, vitality, and growth.

Planting Sunflower Seeds for Personal Growth

Sunflowers can be planted after the threat of frost has passed in your area and preferably after the soil has warmed up a bit. The warmer the soil is, the better the results. Even in the Midwest, sunflowers can be planted as late as June, which will have them blooming and ripe just in time for Mabon! Whenever you choose to plant your sunflowers, you can easily turn it into a magickal event.

To turn your sunflower planting into spellwork, you'll need:

• Biodegradable paper

• Biodegradable ink

• An essential oil you associate with growth (Recommended oils include patchouli, pine, neroli, and myrrh.)

• Sunflower seeds and a place to plant them

To start, think about what you would like to bring into your life over the next three to four months. Write it down on a small piece of paper while visualizing that outcome in your mind's eye. Around whatever it is that you want to bring into your life, draw symbols and designs you associate with that idea. If, for example, you were looking to grow closer to your Craft practice, you could write down "Witchcraft," and around that word draw small pentagrams and symbols representing deities, the Wheel of the Year, and whatever else is important to you in your practice.

When you are done writing on your piece of paper, draw an invoking pentagram upon it with the oil you have selected and say:

> By the power of love and light,
> What I want is in my sight:
> My goal through magick power
> And the growth of the sun's flower!

Now pick up your sunflower seeds and hold them in your dominant hand along with your piece of paper. As you hold them, visualize your end goal. Imagine that goal growing in strength and potency over the summer as your sunflowers (or sunflower) grow. Pour your will and desires into your seeds and paper while chanting:

The spell begun,
My will be done.

When you feel the seeds in your hand pulse with magickal energy, stop the chanting and take them outside to be planted. If you are planting a lot of sunflowers, you can repeat this operation several times using multiple pieces of paper and seeds.

Once outside, place the piece of paper with your intention under the seeds while continuing to visualize what it is you are trying to bring into your life. Hold that visualization until everything has been put into the soil. Once you are done with the planting, stand up and say:

Power of life, power of sun,
With these seeds, my will be done!
Bring forth what I desire,
Through air, rain, earth, and fire!

Over the course of the next few months, check in on your plants daily. As they grow, they will release your intent out into the universe so it can manifest. To raise the energy of the spell, repeat the above phrase every so often while visualizing your end goal. (Be sure to change the word "seeds" to "sprouts" and later "plants.") Higher concentrations of magickal energy will be released when your sunflowers bloom.

Charge Your Magickal Jewelry

Did you know that the heads of sunflowers follow the path of the sun throughout the day? That's right: the heads of sunflowers actually move from east to west! You can use this to your advantage if you need to charge an item, particularly magickal jewelry. I know that in the summer especially, I'm run pretty ragged and could always use a bit of extra energy and vitality. I do this magickally by harvesting the power of the sun via the sunflowers in my backyard.

Choose an item you want to charge and make sure it's something you can easily attach to a piece of string or a necklace. Next, take it outside as close to sunrise as possible and secure it to the top of your tallest sunflower. Generally there's a stem and a leaf right under the bloom of a sunflower, which is where you want to place your item. Once it's there, look at your sunflower while feeling the sun's rays on you and say:

> By *the shining sun's eternal power,*
> I *charge this (item) by light and flower.*
> *May it give me strength and vitality,*
> *Through earth and sky, so mote it be!*

Any item you place on your sunflower will absorb some energy from both the flower and the sun. Wear that particular charm when you need an extra boost or when you know that you've got a long day ahead of you.

Sunflower Seeds for Home Protection

I sometimes think of the sunflowers in my backyard as my garden's protectors. They stand large and proud in the back row of my garden, looking out into the world. Those flowers generally survive strong winds, early rains, and even the ravages of snails and squirrels. There's something powerful about sunflowers, which is why I use their seeds in a yearly protection spell around my house. The average sunflower head can easily produce over a thousand seeds, so each year I have enough seeds to do some magick and ensure a fresh crop of sunflowers for the following year.

I sometimes think of the sunflowers in my backyard as my garden's protectors.... There's something powerful about sunflowers, which is why I use their seeds in a yearly protection spell around my house.

For this spell, wait until your flowers are mature and the seeds are ready to be harvested, generally about 110 days after they first break through the ground. Depending on the size of your yard, you'll probably need fifty to a hundred seeds, and lots more if you have acres of ground to protect! Gather your seeds and place them in a small bowl. Set the bowl on your working altar (or, better yet, a pentacle on your altar), and invoke into your seeds the powers of earth and sun, Goddess and God, and all that lies between those polarities:

> By the power of the noonday sun, sentinel of the skies,
> By the power of my garden's flowers, my magickal allies,
> By the power of the Goddess fair, mother to us all,
> By the power of the Horned One, deity of the fall,
> By the power of what lies between, all that I surmise,
> Safety, protection, hearth, and home, these I visualize!
> May my home be safe from intruder, weather, and harm.
> In that work, these seeds shall be my charm!
> Powers of the universe, through my seeds come to me.
> The spell now cast, my will be done, and so mote it be!

As you say this invocation, you should feel energy rushing into your seeds. While saying these words, be sure to visualize your home safe from threats during the coming winter months. Once your seeds are charged, walk around the perimeter of where you live and scatter the seeds at the boundaries. For extra protection, I sometimes sprinkle extra seeds outside the doors and windows of my home. As you scatter your seeds, say:

By *the power of these seeds,*
Evil shall let me be!

When you are done, thank the sunflowers you've grown and set some seeds aside so you can do this again next year.

Jason Mankey *first tried to grow sunflowers in Michigan. He finally succeeded after moving to California. He's the author of* The Horned God of the Witches *and* Witch's Wheel of the Year. *He has been practicing Witchcraft for over twenty-five years and lives in the Bay Area with his wife, Ari, and two cats.*

Illustrator: Rik Olson

Thinking Magically: Weaving Magic into Your Day with Affirmations

Durgadas Allon Duriel

Look around yourself for a moment and reflect on what exists because of thought. The furniture in our rooms, our technological devices, the structures of our homes, the vehicles we drive—all of these began as ideas that eventually found their way to manifestation through human ingenuity.

Now consider the core elements of your reality that you can't see that also exist because of thought. Your name, for example, is a combination of sounds that have meaning rooted in thought;

and language itself, in its ability to convey abstraction, is the product of thought. The country you live in, in terms of its government, social systems, etc., came into existence because of thoughts, and continues to exist because of them.

I call this type of reality thought-dependent reality, because it depends on thought to exist. If we stop thinking it into being, it will disappear from our experience. When a group of people collectively agree that something that depends on thought to exist is real—like a nation or its laws—they create a shared reality, called a consensus reality. When a critical mass of them determines that this thought-dependent element of reality has changed or stopped being real, it shifts or fades accordingly.

As we number the elements of our experience that are thought-dependent, it becomes clear that much of our reality, and what comprises our everyday lives, is thought into being. The fact that we aren't aware of this happening, and that we can instantly recognize and understand thought-dependent things without having to consciously think about them (like knowing how to drive, use a computer, or what a friend's name is) tells us that the process by which thought-dependent reality is created, moment by moment, is largely subconscious and automatic. We know it occurs, though, because at some point none of these thought-dependent elements existed for us. We were born with clear minds and told to believe that certain things were true of reality. As we believed those things were real, we began to perceive reality accordingly, alongside other elements we came to understand as real through observation.

Many of us have experienced a less expansive version of this process as adults when starting a new job or joining a religious movement and witnessing our perceptions change as we acclimate to the novel circumstance. For instance, as we take on new beliefs about morality from joining a religion, behaviors that may have felt fine to us in the past might now make us cringe. This shift is purely mental,

yet it has powerful emotional and perceptual effects, which automatically occur once the subconscious mind has digested and affirmed this change's reality.

Introducing Affirmations

What this all means in a nutshell is that when we believe something is real on a subconscious level, it becomes real for us. Even if it lacks physical manifestation, it is a substantial part of our experience. In other words, a thought that we believe represents reality shapes or creates within our reality. The name for a thought used intentionally toward these ends is an *affirmation*, which brings us to the central topic here (and the process we've just reviewed sheds light on why affirmations are so powerful and magical on a psychological level).

Though an affirmation technically is any thought performed with the intent to change or create within our reality, affirmations are popularly presented as being positive, sweeping statements that help us heal, develop, and manifest, such as "I love and approve of myself" and "Money comes to me freely and easily." Because of this precedent, I think it's important to emphasize that other thoughts qualify as affirmations too. Prayer is affirmation, for instance, because it shapes our reality to cultivate a relationship with the divine. A goal is an affirmation because it declares an intention to manifest or interact with reality in alignment with our thinking.

Whenever we think, we participate in the process of creating and shaping our perception of reality with thought. Even seemingly insignificant thoughts create within our experience, though the most powerfully creative thoughts are those with an emotional charge. When these thoughts generally reinforce what we already believe, this creative process will be difficult to observe. When they don't, our creative power becomes more apparent. The key for these shifts is for the thoughts to permeate the subconscious mind. One way to assess if this has happened is through observing what we perceive and feel.

As we navigate our everyday lives, we have knee-jerk emotional reactions to events. When this occurs, we can usually see that we're holding a belief or beliefs in our subconscious mind that inspired the emotional reaction. Sometimes these beliefs align with what we consciously think, while other times they may not. For example, someone who has a deep-seated belief that men are threatening may react to men they don't know with panic. They may even intellectually recognize that most men aren't dangerous, yet still experience this reaction. In these cases, when we have a belief in our conscious mind that differs from what we believe subconsciously, my experience is that the subconscious belief usually holds far more power over our perception of reality and emotional experience.

If we want to create change in our lives regarding what we perceive and how we react emotionally, we must shift the contents of the subconscious. We can do this by affirming a new thought with the aim of it becoming a belief.

Consequently, if we want to create change in our lives regarding what we perceive and how we react emotionally, we must shift the contents of the subconscious. We can do this by affirming a new thought with the aim of it becoming a belief, using the process shared later in this article. Additionally, I find this works best by not only deciding to believe something new and affirming it, but also challenging the beliefs we hold that don't support our desired change. When we affirm new thoughts consistently and challenge those that don't

It's also important to be aware of what thoughts we tend to have and what the logical effects of those thoughts are, and to think in alignment with what we hope to create in our lives.

support them, they soak into our subconscious mind, eventually taking root there. Once they've done that, our reactions to things start shifting accordingly.

Generally speaking, it's also important to be aware of what thoughts we tend to have and what the logical effects of those thoughts are, and to think in alignment with what we hope to create in our lives. This is all without avoiding or denying difficult emotions or circumstances, which is another topic, but one I explore in my book *The Little Work: Magic to Transform Your Everyday Life*. With the thoughts we think that don't support our well-being and intentions and seem skewed, we can question their accuracy to dismantle them. For instance, a thought like "Nothing ever works out for me" is probably untrue, but many of us have thoughts like that and feel that way accordingly. So our first step can be to explore this thought with questions like, "What effect does believing this thought have on me?" and "Why might this thought not be true?" After that, we can design a supportive affirmation to begin replacing our old thought using the process shared below.

So far, we've only explored how thought creates reality on the psychological level. There is also the metaphysical level, which is where we discover the notion that our thoughts influence what manifests within our reality. Though this topic is complex (and I explored it in depth in my book), fundamentally, when we think in support of the manifestation of certain intentions, we rally metaphysical forces to aid in manifesting those intentions. Magic isn't just spellwork and ritual. It's also how we think day by day, whether we use our mindset to align with the creations we intend or not. When we're aligned, our intentions tend to manifest more readily. When we're misaligned, it's more unlikely that they'll pan out.

Affirmations in Practice

Affirmation practice has helped me in many ways. In general, training myself to be more compassionate in my thinking—which to me means being more empathetic, wise, accurate, and fact-oriented—has aided me in healing from traumatic experiences and cultural conditioning that left me with low self-esteem and unhealthy relationship tendencies. This is not as much about particular thoughts I affirmed, although it has involved that, but is more about shifting the overall thought patterns by recognizing old stories playing out in my emotions and behaviors, challenging them, and then affirming compassionate sentiments in their place.

For example, I used to believe that something would always sabotage my success. I believed this because, after some traumatic experiences growing up, I felt like I was fundamentally flawed and didn't deserve to be happy or successful. Importantly, I didn't believe this consciously. My conscious thoughts of myself were loaded with insulating defenses. But when I analyzed the emotions I felt in reaction to the events of my life, and what I expected to happen in relationships and in general for me, it was clear that something was off with the deeper levels of my beliefs.

With introspection, I was able to recognize these negative beliefs in myself, and with affirmation practice, plant something else in their place. This old programming didn't always go away completely, but even when it didn't, it became an echo of what it was before, and that's often how this process unfolds. We chip away at beliefs that don't support our well-being and incrementally progress over time.

Weaving Magic with Affirmations

I also planted affirmations in support of the magic I was working, and this is one way we can weave magic into our day with them. When we know that our thoughts are part of our magical process, we can use them accordingly. If we're trying to manifest something specific, we can make an affirmation about that. If we want to manifest a general quality in our lives, we can make an affirmation about that too.

Affirmations also help us weave magic into our days through reminding us that thought is magical, that what we water in the gardens of our minds grows. If we want to be and feel more compassionate, abundant, grateful, and prosperous, it's important to think in a manner that fosters that. As our thoughts align with those sentiments, our subconscious will get on board. When that happens, we find support for our magic even without consciously thinking about it.

As I mentioned earlier, there are many ways to engage in affirmation practice, some of which are more fruitful than others depending on our individual constitution. Generally, traditional affirmations are phrased in the present tense, with the idea being that if we want our reality to take a certain form, we must affirm that it already is like that. Otherwise, we can push our desired reality into the future indefinitely. For instance, if I affirm, "I will be healed," then that could happen in twenty years or more. Conversely, "I am healed" happens now.

The problem with this approach, which many have experienced as they've tried it, is that if we don't believe we're healed, significant emotional stress can accompany this practice. That stress then works against the effectiveness of the affirmation because more often than not, it reinforces our doubt in the change. A work-around I use and recommend for this is to affirm in an incremental fashion, such that each affirmation doesn't require us to leap so far from where we are emotionally. With this system, you create an affirmation along a theme of desired change, and as each affirmation feels true to you, you create a new one closer to where you seek to go. For example, if "I love and approve of myself" feels far-fetched, we can start with "I have admirable qualities," which we affirm until it feels true. Next, we may try something like "Everyone deserves love, including me," and so on.

Designing Affirmations

Here is a process for designing affirmations. As a reminder, we can also create affirmations that are more like prayer or to support our spiritual beliefs (e.g., "The divine is within all things," "May my work serve the highest good," etc.) to increase their presence in our conscious mind and perceptions.

1. Identify a belief you want to change (e.g., "I'm not worth anything.").

2. Identify the theme(s) of this belief (e.g., a sense of value).

3. Identify the spectrum of feelings that encapsulate this theme (e.g., "I feel valueless" to "I'm indisputably valuable.").

4. Use your feelings to locate your current position along this spectrum (e.g., "I feel like I have some worth.").

5. Design an affirmation that's an emotional step above that (e.g., "My self-worth can develop from where I am."). Avoid including unwanted conditions in your affirmation, as that can reinforce them in your experience (e.g., rather than "I'm stronger than anxiety," affirm, "I'm strong enough to face what comes to me.")

6. Recite this affirmation four or more times a day until it feels true. Then create a new one that's closer to where you want to progress with this issue (e.g., "My self-worth grows daily.").

My experience with affirmations is that as we make them part of our everyday lives, we experience their flowering more frequently. You don't need to take my word for it that they're magical, though. You will see for yourself as you practice them diligently. And, in my experience, the more we get a sense that our thoughts are magical, the more we begin to think in a magical way overall—in a manner that creates with intent, rather than simply because it is the nature of thought to manifest realities.

Durgadas Allon Duriel (San Francisco Bay Area, CA) *is the author of* The Little Work: Magic to Transform Your Everyday Life *and a formal practitioner of magic with more than twenty years of experience. He has been an initiate of the Hermetic mysteries since 2005, a journey that began with two and a half years of intensive training. Durgadas is also a licensed clinical social worker and a certified holistic health practitioner, and he has studied and practiced yoga for over sixteen years. Visit him online at durgadasallonduriel.com.*

Illustrator: Bri Hermanson

Creating a Magickal Kitchen

Gwion Raven

When I picture witchcraft, the actual *doing* of witchcraft, I see cauldrons bubbling and jars filled with rare and exotic ingredients. There's a witch hunched over a countertop grinding herbs in a mortar with a pestle. In a book that lies open, frequently used spells are easily identifiable by the blood- and spice-stained pages. Strange and glorious scents waft through the air. When the witch is finished, a devilishly delectable dish finds its way to a table. Waiting and perhaps unsuspecting guests polish off the meal only to realize that everything they ate was part of a spell. Every

bite, every slurp, even the napkins and the silverware were enchanted. Their minds and bodies are fully infused as the magick begins to work.

Or maybe I just served you a bowl of pasta with my favorite Bolognese sauce, made from scratch. You see, I'm a kitchen witch, and there's magick in everything I cook.

Although the description above sounds like something out of a fairy tale, it's a pretty accurate description of me in the kitchen. Saucepans and Dutch ovens are my cauldrons. I really do own an unwieldy number of jars brimming with spices and herbs and seeds and nuts and…well, it's a lot. That bit about food being a spell and witching the forks? It's true. Everything in my kitchen has a magickal purpose, even the very room itself.

Most every day I'm in the kitchen working my way through a new recipe or sharpening knives or wondering what to do with potatoes that I haven't done a thousand times before. It's easy to get jaded after washing dishes for the umpteenth time. But then it hits me like the proverbial lightning bolt and I remember why I spend hours shopping and chopping and pricing and slicing: The human beings in my life need food to live. If they don't eat and drink, they will cease to be, and in pretty short order, too. When I cook a meal, I'm saying, "I'm willing to give you some of my curried red lentils, slowly simmered with cumin and ginger and onions, because you are important to me and I want you fed and full and happy." When I cook, it's an expression of love. Fostering love, as clichéd as it sounds, is the absolute best magick I can ever hope to perform.

Becoming a Kitchen Witch: A Ritual in the Time It Takes to Microwave a Cup of Coffee

I'd been cooking for years and years before I decided to call myself a kitchen witch. If someone in my household was feeling ill, I knew instantly which tea to brew to settle their stomach. When a friend got dumped, grilled cheese sandwiches soothed their broken heart. At some point people began asking me for recommendations for special meals to set the mood or to concoct potions for a desired outcome, or they wanted dishes to chase away depression or illness. That's when I realized I was a kitchen witch. I remember standing in my kitchen and saying out loud to whoever was listening in whatever realm they found themselves in, "Well, I guess I should make it official. I am a kitchen witch." And that was that. It was done. So mote it be and pass the cookies.

People began asking me for recommendations for special meals to set the mood or to concoct potions for a desired outcome, or they wanted dishes to chase away depression or illness. That's when I realized I was a kitchen witch.

Here is a slightly more elaborate ritual you can perform to become a kitchen witch. Now, I like a well-planned, thoroughly researched ritual as much as the next person. You know, during the right phase of the moon, on a Tuesday, when the Sun in Taurus is conjunct the Ten of Cups and the cat says it's an auspicious day. Other times, though, magick is about grabbing what's on hand and making a decision. This ritual fits in that category. The entire ritual should take about ninety seconds. Choosing to reheat the morning's coffee in your microwave is totally optional, but it's a useful device for making sure you're not overdoing it. The *ding* of the microwave means the ritual is over.

1. Set aside ninety seconds.

2. Find yourself in the place where you cook most often (which could be in the kitchen, near the grill on your patio, or in front of the shared hotplate in your communal kitchen).

3. Turn a full 360 degrees, and as you do, say:

I am a kitchen witch. Magick happens here.

I am a kitchen witch. Magick moves through my hands and my tools.

I am a kitchen witch. Magick heals and binds and protects and brings love and keeps away the unwanted.

I am a kitchen witch. Magick is stirred and chopped and brewed and frozen and canned and eaten and savored and shared. I am a kitchen witch.

Depending on your circumstances, I recommend proclaiming this out loud three times, with your voice getting stronger and stronger with each recitation.

Turning Your Kitchen into a Temple— Because Temples Are Power Centers

As I look back, there are a handful of really special sites where I've delved into life-changing and profound magic. There's a redwood forest in Northern California that hosts a private gathering of witches nearly every year. Folks in the know call it "camp." Nestled at the base of a snow-capped mountain in Washington state is an organic farm. Friends of mine call it the "stone circle." There's a twelve-by-twelve-foot spare room in an ordinary house not far from where I live that transforms into a safe haven for a small coven of witches. It's known simply as the "ritual room."

The names aren't grandiose, but what's important is that the places have names associated with magick. Invoking the name of a place brings it alive. When I think of the ritual room, I picture the people

I'm there with, the candles, the altar, and the magick we do. It's like I'm there. I'm connected to the place and to the magick and to the people, and I draw strength from those connections.

Those places are more than their physical features. Through use and intention and magick, they are transformed into temples, and temples are places of power. Which brings me to the kitchen.

My kitchen is not fancy at all. I have a fridge, a basic gas stove and oven, decent counter space, and a sink. There's a pretty cool spice rack, a thrift-store-find pine cabinet stuffed with jars of herbs, and cast-iron pots, pans, and Dutch ovens I've collected over the years. The most "chefy" thing in my kitchen are my knives, which I love. But when I step into my kitchen, it's like the rest of the house fades away. As I cross the threshold from the dining room into the kitchen, the four walls seem to elongate. There is plenty of space, all the time I need, and a sense of calm there. There is no place I'd rather be. I am safe. I am confident. This space is familiar and welcoming and I do magick here. This is my temple.

The fact that my kitchen is a temple is not an accident. I planned it that way. I did magick to make it so. Here are the magickal steps I first used to establish my kitchen temple space.

The fact that my kitchen is a temple is not an accident. I planned it that way. I did magick to make it so. Here are the magickal steps I first used to establish my kitchen temple space. With the exception of step 1, I do all of these steps at least twice a year as part of my regular magickal upkeep.

Building the Kitchen Temple, Step 1

The first step is to name your kitchen. Call it "My Temple to Cooking" or "Where I Practice Healing" or "Hestia's Roadside Diner." Name it something meaningful to you, but as with any magick, really think about what you're going to call into being. If your kitchen is dubbed "Cerridwen's Cauldron," it's likely you'll be working a lot with transformation, whether you want to or not.

Once you have a name, set a *temenos*, or boundary line. Clearly define where your kitchen begins and ends. You might use sea salt or cascarilla to draw the line. You could sprinkle herbs or just use your finger. It's not important how you draw the boundary, but it is critical that you do it.

Building the Kitchen Temple, Step 2

The next piece of magick involves cleaning the kitchen from top to bottom, including scrubbing and sweeping. Like a task from Baba Yaga, this step is not fun. It's tedious and grueling. You might have to dedicate a whole weekend to doing this, or pay someone to do it, or invite the coven over with the understanding that you'll help them do the same thing one day.

Instead of using commercial products, see if you can use some natural cleaners. I like to put lemons and limes and oranges down the sink. I grind them up in the disposal unit and it smells lovely. I've made natural cleaning sprays by filling a spray bottle with equal parts water and white vinegar. To that I add fifteen drops of essential oil: five drops of lavender, five drops of thyme, and five drops of rosemary. Those are my favorites, and there are some antibacterial components to them too. If those scents aren't your cup of tea, do some research and see which oils appeal to your olfactory senses and have cleaning properties as well.

The last action should be to sweep. Get out your broom and sweep in a deosil (clockwise) fashion, or as close to that as you can. Sweep out the old and make room for the new.

Building the Kitchen Temple, Step 3

After the cleaning comes the cleansing. There's a subtle difference between cleaning and cleansing. The first aligns with hygiene and tidying, while the second is focused more on the ethereal health of your space. Both are important. Since we're building a kitchen temple, I like to bind culinary herbs together into a bundle. I use bay leaves, rosemary, and thyme most often, but I've also used mugwort, lavender, rose petals, basil, and cilantro. Once I have the herbs bundled, I grab a favorite heatproof bowl, light the herbs, and let the smoke permeate the room. Another option is to fill the bowl with salt water and dip the herb bundle into the water. Then use the bundle to sprinkle water about the place. Remember to get the smoke or water into the oven, the cutlery drawer, the cupboard you keep the cereal in, and any areas that open, like windows and vents.

As you cleanse the temple, picture in your witch's eye what your kitchen temple looks like. Is it an old cottage in the woods or a rustic grill over charcoal, or is it what I picture: the gleaming stainless steel cathedral of a modern restaurant kitchen?

Building the Kitchen Temple, Step 4

The final step in creating your kitchen temple involves planting something green and living in the kitchen window. I love having basil or mint in the kitchen. Both herbs are associated with abundance and have a plethora of magickal and culinary uses. But really, any plant will do. If you have trouble keeping plants alive, find a piece of art with plants or herbs in it. After all, your kitchen magick is closely associated with the processes of growing and harvesting and replanting.

Use these ideas to make your kitchen a magical space and manifest magick in the world through food. As you begin to embrace kitchen witchery, you will see that cookery is only one part of the equation.

Gwion Raven *is a tattooed Pagan, writer, traveler, musician, cook, kitchen witch, occult shop owner, and teacher, and the author of* The Magick of Food: Rituals, Offerings & Why We Eat Together. *Although initiated in three magickal traditions, Gwion describes his practice as virtually anything that celebrates the wild, sensuous, living, breathing, dancing, ecstatic, divine experiences of this lifetime. Born and raised in London, he now resides in Northern California and shares space with redwood trees, the Pacific Ocean, and his beloved partner. Visit Gwion at GwionRaven.com and on Instagram @themagickoffood.*

Illustrator: M. Kathryn Thompson

Divination & Signs

Sapphire Moonbeam

As I stood on the ancient grounds at the Temple of Apollo and the Oracle of Delphi on a rocky, steep mountain area in Greece, I imagined what it would have been like to live in that time period. People from Greece and travelers from distant lands had arrived at that very spot after journeying for miles and sometimes days in search of answers. The seekers wanted to get predictions and gain definitive guidance on how to proceed and what to do to prepare for future events in their lives.

History of Divination

Divination has been practiced for centuries. The ancients were in touch with the earth and sky. It was normal and quite practical for them to watch for signs in the natural world. They paid close attention to the stars, the sun and moon, storms, trees, animals, the flight patterns of birds, and even the direction of the wind. Our ancestors were connected to the natural rhythms, signs, guidance, and endless messages from the universe. In the days of old, both commoners and people in powerful positions relied heavily on divination and diviners. They had an unwavering belief in the predictions and signs that were revealed.

The good news is that you don't have to travel to a distant land to seek the predictions of an oracle, seer, or diviner. As a person living in modern times, with access to thousands of books and a vast array of online knowledge at your fingertips, you can find a type of divination that works best for you. Seeing signs through divination and receiving messages from the universe is available to all of us. It only requires that you have an open mind, awareness, a willingness to learn, and the passion to discover the available knowledge about the type of divination that really enchants you. Becoming more awake and spiritually aware of the happenings in nature and your surroundings will lead you to more meaningful and enriching experiences in your daily life. The best part about modern divination is the ability to pair it with your own intuition and your wise inner voice concerning the relevance and truth of the information you receive.

Divination is a quest for answers and a search for greater meaning. It is about seeing signs and symbols and getting some reassurance that our lives are connected to something much bigger than ourselves. Divination can help us discover the next step on the road of our spiritual life path. It is a magical way to obtain divine guidance and shows us how to see a connection between events, people, and places. Divination can provide clues to the knowledge we seek. It can help us feel forewarned, prepared, optimistic, and empowered and can provide us with much needed inspiration and hope as we continue to find our way.

Practicing Divination and Types

When you think about the art of divination, some of the first images that come to mind might be a witch gazing into a crystal ball for visions, a mystic reading tarot or oracle cards for messages, a spiritually awakened soul studying astrology, a magical person reading tea leaves, or an intuitive interpreting the lines in a person's hand during a palm reading. Those are the more common forms of divination, but there are many more types to discover. Finding the type of divination that resonates with you is a fascinating and educational journey. Depending on your level of magical knowledge, you may not realize how many types of divination are available.

You could learn more about the art of casting lots, or cleromancy. This is a method of divination where you toss sand, sticks, or rocks onto the ground and look for patterns. The same thing can be done by rolling dice and utilizing the knowledge of numbers in numerology. The technique of casting lots can be practiced with any type of small handheld objects such as runes, stones, or even bones. There is actually one woman in the UK who does divination with asparagus. She uses the vegetable for casting lots and considers herself the world's only "asparamancer."

Another interesting magical practice is pyromancy, which is the art of recognizing images and patterns in the flames of a fire and even being aware of the color of the smoke. Or perhaps learning more about the magical practice of scrying might appeal to you, where you relax your eyes while looking into a crystal ball for signs and visions. You can also gaze at a blackened mirror in candlelight.

Divination can be used to help you achieve your goals. If you have a big goal you want to reach and are determined and committed to work for it, you can use divination to answer questions about how to get from point A to point B. Instead of just picking a tarot card, oracle card, or rune for the traditional meaning, ask specific questions and request that answers be revealed to you about the best next step on the path toward your goal.

Divination can be used to help you achieve your goals.... Instead of just picking a tarot card, oracle card, or rune for the traditional meaning, ask specific questions and request that answers be revealed to you about the best next step on the path toward your goal.

I love practicing many different types of divination as well as noticing, seeing, and recognizing magical signs from the universe. I find ways to incorporate these practices into my life every day. Nature signs are always around me. The type of divination I choose to use each day depends on what is happening in my life and the reason that I am searching for extra guidance.

Cartomancy is one of my favorite forms of divination. I love consulting tarot, Lenormand, and oracle cards. I most often consult oracle cards to receive lighthearted yet helpful, supportive messages to inspire me. The cards give me a fresh perspective about the situation I am currently facing. Oracle cards usually have a very clear and potent message to share. I pick one oracle card in the morning to help set my intention for the day, and sometimes I choose one card in the evening to reflect on the insights

I received that day. Oracle cards are an easy way for anyone to interpret a message without help from others and without a great deal of study and practice.

If you are drawn to earth energies, like I am, and resonate with the energies of stones and crystals, you can use them for daily divination. Divination with crystals doesn't have to be elaborate or difficult. Obtain a small leather or velvet bag and place crystals of a similar size inside. Create a daily ritual by placing your hand in the bag and rolling the crystals around with your fingers, then pick one crystal each day for a message. The symbolic metaphysical meanings of the crystal you choose can give you clues about what the day may bring, what you need to focus on, and what you need to learn more about. Over time, as you become more familiar with the metaphysical properties of each stone and crystal, you can also create a simple spread like you might use with tarot or oracle cards in order to get more specific meanings and placements, like past, present, and future energies.

Noticing Patterns

As an artist, I am always fascinated by signs in nature, patterns, and the animals that cross my path. I have found that as my spiritual journey has continued to evolve over time, I notice the signs more frequently. I love seeing the various magical signs from the universe. They are always there, just waiting to be noticed.

I remember as a child lying on my back in the grass and looking up at the puffy white clouds floating by in the beautiful blue sky. It was easy to look up and see recognizable shapes in the clouds. As an adult, I still use this technique, since I have never really lost my childlike spirit. If you can reconnect with your inner child, you may also begin seeing more shapes in the clouds. If you see a cloud that looks like a sailboat, it could mean that you are going to embark on a new journey soon. If you notice a cloud that looks like a heart, it could be as simple as the universe reminding you to love yourself more. Looking for recognizable shapes in the sky is simple and available to all of us. The most powerful and magical element in any type of divination is always you.

This simple concept of using my imagination is helpful to me when I do a tea leaf reading. Reading the tea leaves excites me and makes me feel like a mystical detective. I enjoy turning the teacup in various directions so I can see the way the tea leaves form different shapes at different angles. The more creative your mind is, the more possibilities you will see in the tea leaves to determine the message the universe is trying to convey.

Sometimes finding answers can be as simple as asking for a sign to be shown to you and being open-minded and aware enough to see it once it is presented to you. I have seen eyes on the bark of a tree, patterns and shapes in wood flooring, and even an auspicious number of petals on a flower. The universe will find a way to deliver the sign or message in a way that is most meaningful to you.

Animal Spirit and Nature Signs

I recently received a sign from an animal spirit by surprise. I was checking my mailbox and realized the mailbox cover was open. When I reached inside to grab my mail, a large grasshopper greeted me. It jumped and startled me and made me laugh out loud. I had not seen a grasshopper in the area for several years. Later that same day, I saw two more grasshoppers in my backyard. As a fourth sign that day, I received an email from a new friend that had the word "grasshopper" in her email address.

When I see an unusual animal spirit just once in a day, it is something I think about and research. However, seeing the sign three or more times in a single day makes the message more powerful. With the grasshoppers, it was unmistakable to me that there was indeed a message and some wisdom to be gained. I was intrigued, and I took the time to discover the meaning of the grasshopper and meditated on how it related to my life. Seeing the grasshopper sign four times in a day was a crystal-clear message for me. I could not ignore the synchronicity. I believe that any type of repeating, synchronistic sign helps to reinforce the importance of the divinatory message. Seeing this kind of synchronicity also confirms to me that I am on the right path.

Every once in a while, I have seen an unusual animal spirit nature sign. Even if I see it just once, I still know it is significant. For instance, I don't think much of seeing squirrels since they are in my yard every day. However, I recently saw a hummingbird for the first time in my backyard. It flew by me, made a little high-pitched squeak, and fluttered over to a red flower a few feet away. It shocked me and made me gasp, and I was so grateful for the visit. A short time later that same day, I saw a large bright-green caterpillar inching along on a path near my house. It was another thing that I had never seen in my yard. The symbolic meanings of both the hummingbird and the caterpillar were relevant to my circumstances.

Practicing Divination and Journaling

Once you find a form of intentional divination that you are interested in, you need to practice it in order to learn about its symbolism and meanings. A daily practice will help you master the ability to easily interpret the messages. Practicing the divination form you have chosen will help you become intimately familiar with it. Do not become discouraged if it is challenging to learn in the beginning. Divination becomes easier in time.

To keep track of your divinatory messages, you might consider writing in a divination journal. You can record the date, the type of divination used, the card that appeared, and the rune, nature sign, spirit animal, etc., along with a brief description of the message. Your first impression of a message and meaning might be interpreted differently once more time has passed. Journaling will help you recognize patterns of signs showing up more than once, and when you look back on a message, you may discover how it helped predict a future event or led you to a solution to a problem.

A Few More Things to Consider

There may be times in your life when you are too close to a situation or too emotionally involved to be able to interpret objectively the messages you receive from divination. In that case, you might consider asking a trusted friend for help or seek the guidance of a tarot reader or psychic. Once you get their advice, be sure to use your own discernment, and do not allow their predictions to be considered the absolute, unwavering truth.

You are the most magical and powerful element in your life. Keep in mind that you should never give away your personal power while practicing divination and interpreting signs. You always have free will to make choices that will affect your present and your future. Divination signs are guideposts and suggestions on the journey. Trust the signs and the path that feels best to you. Seek the guidance of divination, but be sure to consult the wisdom you already have within.

Sapphire Moonbeam *is a rainbow-inspired energy artist, metaphysical jewelry maker, and nature photographer, as well as a crystal, flower, fairy, and tree lover. She is the artist and author of the Moonbeam Magick oracle card deck. Sapphire teaches intuitive abstract art classes in the Kansas City area, and also teaches at locations around the world. She travels with women's spiritual retreats and connects with the mystical energies at ancient sites in Egypt, Greece, India, Peru, Scotland, Turkey, and more. She has a worldwide following at her Sapphire's Moonbeams page on Facebook. Visit her website at SapphireMoonbeam.com.*

Illustrator: Tim Foley

Small Moments of Magic

Blake Octavian Blair

When we think about magic and the practice of it in our lives, the first visions that are conjured up in our minds are often those of grand ritual dramas created in circles with our covens and groves or at festivals under moonlit skies or in beautiful sunlit pastures—those situations where the magical energy crackles and builds to a crescendo. Or perhaps we focus on grand results, envisioning large financial windfalls or the obtaining of a romantic partner. However, these are not the majority of magical experiences in our lives. Most of our practices manifest more often as what I like to term "small moments of magic."

Small moments of magic are no less powerful or magical than grander ones. In fact, they may be more powerful in their simplicity and directness. The little moments are arguably more important, as they occur every day and frequently at the times when we are most vulnerable and free. Often it is just us standing before our altar or perhaps under a tree in the woods or a park. The moment occurs between us and All That Is. All of us who strive to live a magical life are likely experiencing these moments in our daily lives, so let's take a closer look at exactly what these small moments of magic often look like.

Most of us, at least daily, take a moment to ground and center ourselves in front of our altar. What this looks like will depend on your particular tradition and practice. As part of my daily practice, I have a particular set of practices and prayers I like to do that come from my druidic and shamanic traditions. The nice thing about it is that I can do the long form, which takes about ten to fifteen minutes, or I can do the short form if needed, which takes only about three to five minutes. Whether you take a few moments at the start of your day for a quick prayer and a smudge, or it's midday and you take a few moments to say a little chant and ground and center yourself, those few moments working what could be considered "small" magic can have a huge impact on your overall mood.

Spontaneously Prepared for Magic

Sometimes we plan our small moments of magic, like morning or mealtime prayers, daily healing practices, or casting simple spells. However, a large portion of the time, small moments of magic spontaneously present themselves in the course of our day-to-day lives. There is the moment right before you pull your car out of the driveway and you instinctively utter a prayer for safe travel, or the interaction you

have with a tree that calls to you as you're out in nature, or perhaps that moment when your toes are buried in the sand as the ocean washes up over your feet and you feel a connection with the spirits of the sea. Magical moments are not always the moments we create but instead are the seizing of moments given to us.

The Divine, however you see it, can leave us in awe in these moments, and a seasoned practitioner will take full advantage of them. The longer you have been on your spiritual path, the more connected you will likely feel and the more prepared you will be to respond spontaneously. That sounds like an oxymoron, I realize. How can one be prepared to respond spontaneously? First of all, just by being in the moment. I can hear you asking, "But how?" Well, it is not something that can be explained but rather is learned over time.

In your practice you gradually build a spiritual toolbox of techniques, prayers, invocations, and ways of working with spirit and energy. So you will have the items in your toolbox to call upon naturally and without hesitation at the right time when these [small magical] moments occur for you.

As for being prepared, what I mean by that is that in your practice you gradually build a spiritual toolbox of techniques, prayers, invocations, and ways of working with spirit and energy. So you will have the items in your toolbox to call upon naturally and without hesitation at the right time when these moments occur for you. Perhaps you have a blessing for trees that you learned in your tradition, and when you happen upon a tree that strikes you in a particular way, you are able to recite and confer that blessing. You might then also leave a small (earth-friendly) offering from a bag you've come to always carry with you. That small and quiet moment occurred spontaneously and likely lasted but a fleeting minute or three; however, it was in the making for quite some time as you learned while walking your path.

When you are out and about in nature, pay attention and tune in to the life around you. Let your sixth sense guide you. Many magical practitioners tell stories of having a flash of intuition and then seeing an animal dart across their path or a significant bird land in a tree. Some of these moments are surely messages and omens. But some of them, of course, are not grand divinatory omens or messages. Over time, you'll learn to distinguish between the two. For example, you'll notice that you are drawn to some trees over others. I do not mean simply species, but individual trees as well. You will know when a tree has a message for you as opposed to when it is just sharing sacred space with you.

It is important to recognize that the occurrences that bring us omens and messages and the ones that do not are both sacred and magical in their own way. Sometimes you simply happen to be in the same space with a being—in the same forest as a majestic old tree, in a field with beautiful wildflowers, or on a nature trail when a fox crosses your path. Even when the being does not have a specific message for you, you are still sharing sacred space. (Isn't all of nature sacred, not just the places where we cast our circles?) You are standing upon the same ground as the tree, exchanging air with the wildflowers, treading the same forest glen as the fox. You are sharing sacred space and the elements together. These are the magical moments of being alive and part of the interconnected web of being.

One of the most treasured holiday traditions I share with my husband is getting up to watch the sunrise on the winter solstice. It's a big moment of astronomical proportions. However, we celebrate in "small moment" style. We trek to a nice outdoor viewing location, with a thermos of hot coffee libation along for the ride. We like to be in our chosen location about thirty minutes prior to sunrise. We dress in full New England winter ritual regalia. This generally consists of long underwear, a wool coat, and hand-knit caps and mittens, topped off with a hand-knit scarf or cowl. At the moment of sunrise, we greet the rising sun with a prayer and the shaking of bell branch rattles, then finish with the chanting of Awen. The rattles have a gentle, magical sound and the chanting is calming and resonant. Once indoors, where it is a little less frosty, mimosas are a wonderful solar-associated post-ritual drink.

Small but Significant

Most people in magical spiritualities find themselves engaged in healing work at some point or another. Whether it is Reiki for yourself, just the occasional healing candle for a friend, or perhaps distance healing for others, these practices often qualify as small moments of magic. I think most of us can relate to being asked, sometimes rather unexpectedly, to send healing or say a prayer for a person in need. The course of action may be to simply light a candle and say a prayer at your altar, or you might send distance Reiki. The amount of time you spend on the task will vary, but this will likely not be a grand ritual drama with a lot of flash.

However, for some of us, healing work may be one of our most common practices. I am frequently asked to do a shamanic journey on behalf of someone. Oftentimes it does not look like much outwardly as I sit or lie down and travel by drumbeat into the Otherworlds. Many times, if there are any onlookers, there isn't a great deal for them to see for the majority of the work. However, I have a great deal of gratitude for the helping spirits and what I've seen them accomplish.

It is likely apparent to you by now that the word *small* is not used here to denote a level of power or importance. In fact, such moments can be some of the most potent experiences! The word also is not necessarily used to denote a specific duration of time. Rather, I am using the term *small* as an umbrella descriptor to encapsulate those quiet, simpler, sometimes spontaneous, and often semi-private magical and spiritual occurrences that happen to us in the everyday world.

> **Embracing the small moments of magic can lead us to deepen the presence of our spirituality in the everyday tasks we already engage in....There is seemingly no better solution than finding ways to make the activities you already engage in a part of your spiritual practice.**

Well, the everyday world of the magical practitioner. I'm not sure how many other people who live on my street can be found on any given day rattling and whistling with gusto, calling upon their power animals (perhaps proving that these moments are not always quiet and they might have some flair to them on occasion).

Embracing the small moments of magic can lead us to deepen the presence of our spirituality in the everyday tasks we already engage in. In an era when people often lament being so busy that they don't know how they can ever find time to be spiritual and engage in a daily practice, there is seemingly no better solution than finding ways to make the activities you already engage in a part of your spiritual practice.

A simple case in point is your morning coffee or tea—a ritual many of us not only engage in daily but also wouldn't miss for the world! In the ritual preparation of your morning drink, consider the plant spirits that provided the drink, where they came from, and what magical qualities they lend. As you stir in sugar, milk or cream, honey, etc., do it with intention. You are literally brewing and stirring a small cauldron in that mug, after all! Since you're already engaging in the motions of ritual spellcraft, you might as well make it real and put energy and intention into it. All of a sudden your morning drink is now a magical potion.

An important thing to remember is that small moments of magic, much like grander ones, can take time to manifest. As anyone on the path for a length of time will admit, magic takes patience. Most magic isn't a "one and done" experience. Energy and intention are built over time. If you are working with deities or spirits, this definitely applies, as relationships are built over time. Results take time to manifest, and often energy to maintain once achieved. So one practice you might take up that fits the "small moments of magic" philosophy is that of magical or spiritual journaling. Maybe you do this daily, or perhaps less frequently. What is important is that you do it on a regular basis. Each session may take only a handful of minutes, and you can even bullet-journal. Do not feel as though your journaling needs to amount to the quantity of writing required for a novel! Journal daily, twice-weekly,

> **Small moments of magic, much like grander ones, can take time to manifest.... Magic takes patience. Most magic isn't a "one and done" experience. Energy and intention are built over time.**

or weekly, whatever works for you. The important thing is that the habit needs to be pretty regular to be of benefit, so you can notice trends and results as you look back over entries. Over time, you may detect trends and changes developing that indicate results that are so gradual that you may not have noticed them from day to day. It's a lovely confirmation of the fruits of your spiritual labors.

Shared Small Moments

There is another way that small moments add up to big results: through collective group efforts. Both healing and social justice energy work and magic are great examples of this. Perhaps a person in your community is in need of healing, and you arrange for a number of members in your spiritual community to perform the same healing spell for the person. This collective effort, with each individual putting their drop into the cauldron, has the potential to combine for big results! The "rolling thunder" style of healing rituals that are popular in the pagan community are another example of this. In this type of working, all individuals send healing energy at a set time, in their own time zone, creating a continuous wave of energy. Similar efforts can be enacted for social justice work, with appropriate spellwork designed for collective efforts.

I happen to be the Abbot and co-organizer of a Brigidine flame-keeping cill. Our Abbess, and my co-organizer, is witchy woman and fellow author Mickie Muller. We organize a total of nineteen flame-keepers (the two of us included) in a traditional twenty-day cycle to tend Brigid's eternal flame. Each flamekeeper's shift consists of what most would consider small moments of magic. The vigil of keeping the flame involves a twenty-four-hour shift, once every twenty days for each participant, during which the flamekeeper makes prayers and does healing work and perhaps divination. However, this vigil work is mostly done while the flamekeeper goes about their daily life.

A flamekeeping shift is not twenty-four hours of solid monastic meditation; it is a mindful day spent engaging in mostly small moments of magic. However, it adds up to the large collective result of Brigid's flame being perpetually maintained by being energetically passed among all nineteen members, and tended by Brigid herself on the twentieth day.

Drops in the Cauldron

When you are searching for ways to live a more magical life or deepen your spirituality, do not fret, for opportunities are all around you. You need only find those small moments to savor: the prayer of gratitude for the sweet parts of life while stirring honey into your tea, the magic of realizing you are sharing the air you breathe with the hawk soaring overhead, or the calming message of reassurance you receive from a tree. Hopefully this short article will help spark practices of your own that bring magic into your life. Remember, small drops added to the cauldron can add up to create big splashes! Don't be afraid to think big and act small...and engage in a few small moments of magic today.

Blake Octavian Blair *is a shamanic and druidic practitioner, ordained minister, writer, Usui Reiki Master-Teacher, tarot reader, and musical artist. He incorporates mystical traditions from both the East and the West with a reverence for the natural world into his own brand of spirituality. Blake holds a degree in English and religion from the University of Florida. He is an avid reader, knitter, crafter, and member of the Order of Bards, Ovates & Druids. He loves communing with nature and exploring its beauty, whether it is within the city or while hiking in the woods. Blake lives in the New England region of the US with his beloved husband. Visit him on the web at www.blakeoctavianblair.com.*

Illustrator: Rik Olson

Flexibility & Adaptability in Magical Work

Cerridwen Iris Shea

Change and chaos. That's what the last few cycles have brought us. There's been a great deal of hardship and loss in the world in recent years. Yet as magical people, we can dig into the resources from our training and practices to find the flexibility and adaptability we need to survive and to thrive. Flexibility in our magical work can translate to the rest of our lives and help us through rough patches.

There are paths that require the practitioner to use exact wording and follow all portions of a ritual explicitly. I respect those paths. Learning precision is a positive. But when life throws you unexpected challenges, flexibility and adaptability can make all the difference.

It starts with the little things, like forgetting an item in a ritual and making a last-minute adjustment. I've forgotten the salt in an outdoor ritual and used dirt. I've had no access to salt or dirt and used carpet fibers or a wooden pencil to represent earth. The ritual still worked. Sometimes we forget the words to an incantation and have to come up with an alternative. Creating a living, growing, realistic practice will prepare us for the bigger obstacles we're bound to encounter.

As with everything, balance matters. Know when to stick to the plan and when to think on your feet. Now more than ever, we need to create our traditions and maintain our rituals and purposes while still being flexible and adaptive.

Seasons

Let's start with the root of our practice: the cycles of the seasons. Birth, growth, death, renewal. The tree bursts into bloom, it flourishes, it drops its leaves, it rests in the snow, it buds again in spring. We celebrate the maiden's journey into mother and crone and her rebirth into the maiden the following spring. We celebrate the battles between the Holly King and the Oak King, and honor each one's victory. We burn a bonfire on the Summer Solstice, the shortest night of the year, to keep the dark away for just a few more moments before the wheel turns again and the darkness grows longer. We hang lights and ornaments and burn another fire on the Winter Solstice, the longest night, to remind us that the wheel is about to turn back to the light.

We observe the cycles of the moon and the seasons and feel their rhythms. We start projects on the new moon, complete what's in progress on the full moon, and cut away what we no longer need during the waning moon. We plant seeds at the optimal time; we nurture

and we harvest. We keep careful notes and learn as much from our mistakes as from our successes. Even more important, we apply what we've learned, so the following year's harvest is even better than the previous year's crops.

Seasonal Exercise

Buy a packet of perennial seeds or a small perennial plant. At the appropriate time in the season and the moon cycle, plant the seeds or bless the plant. For one year, chart its progress at least once a week in a notebook and with a photograph. Create a collage of photos at the end of the year. Since the plant is a perennial, try charting it again for another year. See how it grows and changes. See how sometimes it works hard and sometimes it needs to rest. Use it as part of your ritual work where appropriate.

If the plant doesn't survive, that, too, is part of the cycle. Thank the plant for your time together and dispose of it with respect.

Decide When You Need a Schedule and When to Throw It Out

There are times when a to-do list gives us a sense of accomplishment as we cross off each item. But other times, even looking at such a list can lead us into despair.

Where do routines and schedules enhance your life? With my latest set of rescued cats, who were moved from household to household for eighteen months before they came to live with me, routine steadied them. Their morning and evening routines are what make them feel safe and grounded. In the mornings, I get up, put on the coffee, feed them, write, do my yoga and meditation, then start my day. The evening ritual is about picking up the bowls to wash them and giving them their bedtime snacks before the nighttime yoga and meditation. When this happens in the same order each morning and evening, they are happy. If something shifts in the routine, they get anxious and fretful and are likely to grumble at each other or get into trouble.

Sharing these routines with them gives me structure and enjoyment to start and end my days. I enjoy their pleasure in the routines. That spiraling pleasure strengthens our bond.

As a freelancer, most of my work is remote and the details of my day often change. This means I can also answer the call of the garden. I have enough flexibility in my day to look out the window and see what the garden needs, then spend some time doing it.

While I weed or battle kudzu or deadhead flowers, I alternate between being in the moment with the plants and working out any stuck places in the day's work. Snipping off a deadheaded flower often makes me realize where I can make a cut in a piece of writing to make it stronger, much as deadheading the plant makes it stronger. The tasks are very different, but they support each other.

> **Snipping off a deadheaded flower often makes me realize where I can make a cut in a piece of writing to make it stronger, much as deadheading the plant makes it stronger. The tasks are very different, but they support each other.**

The garden's needs change as the weather changes. It needs more water if we haven't had rain for a few weeks. This reminds me not to get too rigid or stuck in my routines.

Stress and chaos can disrupt sleep patterns. This became a problem for me during the first stay-at-home weeks of the pandemic in 2020. I started waking up at 2:30 or 3:30 in the morning, no matter what time

I'd gone to bed, and worrying. I would grab my phone, doom-scroll, and feel worse.

After realizing that type of connectivity made me feel isolated instead of comforted, I changed my response to waking up. I chose to sit on my meditation cushion instead of tossing and turning or reaching for the phone.

I sat there, with the discomfort, with the worry, with the fear.

It helped, even when it was uncomfortable.

Sometimes I would settle down enough to realize I was still tired, and go back to bed and manage a few more hours' sleep. If I was truly awake, I would get up and bake bread or start writing. The important part was that I made choices that were positive and active instead of fretting or scrolling. Those choices made me feel better about the upcoming day or week or month, and I was able to meet them with more resilience.

When Something's Not Working, Don't Be Afraid to Change It

The purpose of our magical work is to create a better world for ourselves and those around us. We create spells for protection, for health, for prosperity, for calm. The very nature of what we do is to create positive change. That requires the flexibility to recognize the need for change, the determination to create the change, and the adaptability to work with the process and the result of the change, even when it's not exactly what we expected.

That translates into rituals, too. Sometimes you want the comfort of a ritual you've performed often over the years, and the gathering strength of each repetition. Other times, a ritual that was so perfect for years no longer feels relevant.

That doesn't mean the ritual isn't any good or that you wasted your time. It means that you're growing and your practice needs to grow with you. Put away the rituals that no longer satisfy you. Build time to work on new ritual techniques and changes in your practice that work for you in this moment, which is part of mindfulness practice.

Perhaps you will go back to the earlier rituals at some point when they call to you again. Perhaps you will keep building new rituals. Perhaps you will find ways to merge both. Your growth as a person is interwoven with the growth of your practice. Nothing you try, nothing you work on, is ever wasted. It's all part of growing and building.

Recipe and Spell Adaptation

Most spells published or shared in the community make it clear that the spell is offered as a foundation, and the practitioner is encouraged to adapt the spell as needed. Just as recipes have substitutions, spells can have the same.

One of my favorite substitutions in baking is to replace sugar with honey. I found an online sugar-to-honey converter for proportions. When a recipe calls for sugar, I convert the amount and use honey instead. I started replacing milk with orange juice in some recipes, too. Yes, the taste and texture are different, but that can be wonderful. For me, it's healthier.

Rosemary is my go-to herb. I use it for prosperity, protection, love, healing, and cleansing. When I'm putting together an herbal concoction, I often substitute rosemary for another herb because it resonates so strongly with me and therefore gives my spells a boost.

I like to experiment with recipes so I can cook and bake for friends who are vegan or prefer gluten-free options. Adapting recipes is part of the growth and evolution of palates and health needs and taste cravings, and works on both the magical and the mundane level.

Pull up a favorite spell written by someone else. Perform it once (or once again), exactly as written, and take notes on the experience and how it manifested.

Now decide to make some changes to it. Choose some elements to substitute with items that speak strongly to you. Maybe you need to feel more of a sense of well-being and options in your love spell, so you choose a pink aventurine instead of rose quartz. Or maybe you want to tilt the spell more toward passion, so you use a garnet. Or maybe you want to gently transition out of a love relationship, and use pink Botswana instead of rose quartz to stay in it, or onyx for a clean break.

Perform the ritual again, setting your intent and making note of the substitutions. Make sure to observe and record how it feels, and the results. How did adapting the spell make it more personal? More resonant?

Spontaneity Is Beautiful

One of the wonderful aspects of a long-term magical practice is that certain knowledge, ritual elements, and associations become second nature. This allows us to stand on a beach or in a grove of trees in the forest or in a desert and create spontaneous ritual. The knowledge is in our heartbeat. The tools are in our bodies and minds.

One of the wonderful aspects of a long-term magical practice is that certain knowledge, ritual elements, and associations become second nature.

Sometimes we do spontaneous ritual. After a hike in the woods, we find a gorgeous overlook and breathe gratitude to our gods. Or we go away for the weekend, find a magical spot, and create a ritual in the moment with whatever is on hand: an acorn cap filled with water, a twig, a pebble, a flashlight.

As much as we might love carting around bags of our "stuff" to create outdoor ritual, we don't need it. We can be the ritual, and let ourselves fill with the beauty, gratitude, and joy of the moment. We can laugh and dance as the waves lap our ankles, honoring the sunset, because we are there in the moment, with the moment, and we are living in that moment and are grateful.

Spontaneous Ritual

Go to a favorite place in nature (even if it's in your yard). Don't bring any tools. Take a few deep breaths and find the awareness of place. Now create a ritual in the moment. It doesn't have to be long; it can take only a handful of moments. Just create a ritual of and in the place where you are in that moment.

Record Your Work, Then Reread It to Celebrate Your Progress

Keep detailed records of your rituals and spells. I like to record the date, the moon phase, any planetary retrogrades, and the weather. As you flip back over weeks and months and years of work, you will see how well you've adapted and how much you've grown.

My grimoire (Book of Shadows) is where I write the spells after I've worked on them and performed them enough times to be confident in them. My mirror book is where I track experiments, note changes, and make more frequent notes as I adapt and hone spells, tarot spreads, and so on.

The term *mirror book* has fallen out of favor over the years, but that experimental diary sets the foundation for my grimoire, which contains the polished spells. If I need something tried-and-true and don't have the time or desire to experiment, I reach for my grimoire and flip through it until I find what I need (which is often different from what I think I want). I keep adding to my grimoire as I adapt and hone the spells in my mirror book.

The work feeds the life and the life feeds the work. Together, this tapestry gives us a strong capacity to adapt, survive, and thrive as our realities shift exponentially faster. We are often told not to fear change, but rather to embrace it. That can be difficult, but trusting our work allows us to soar.

Cerridwen Iris Shea *writes, gardens, rescues cats, cooks, reads tarot, and works on spells. She's a hedge witch and a kitchen witch, whether she lives in the city, by the sea, or in the woods. Visit www.cerridwenscottage.com.*

Illustrator: Bri Hermanson

Witchcraft Essentials

PRACTICES, RITUALS & SPELLS

Secondhand Ritual Tools

Lupa

One of the great things about modern Paganism is that it's customizable. Obviously, some cultural practices should be left as is (or, in some cases, not taken out of their original context), but that still leaves plenty of room for individual Pagans to put a personal spin on their practice. We create our own rituals and spells, particularly as we get more experienced, and we have our own relationships with the deities and spirits we work with.

That ability to put a unique spin on one's spirituality certainly extends to ritual tools. In addition to the athame, chalice, wand, and other altar tools commonly found in Wicca and related paths, Pagans may adopt into their ritual gear a variety of statues and images, stones, bones and other natural materials, jewelry, clothing, or even pieces of more advanced technology such as computers. In fact, given the variety of bailiwicks that Pagan deities have, if something exists, there's a good chance someone has used it in rituals or other spiritual practices.

This also means that some Pagans are enthusiastic collectors of ritual tools. You probably know someone with an extensive collection of Tarot decks and other divination tools, or multiple athames and other ritual knives, and perhaps an entire closet full of ceremonial robes and other garb. Given how many artisans, shops, and websites cater to our varied aesthetics, it's fairly easy to find multiple appealing options for any tool you're looking for.

Unfortunately, this can come at a high price in terms of both human rights and the environment. Many of the tools we buy are mass-produced or made from environmentally unsound materials. Take your average candle bought at a dollar store or big-box store, for example. It was made from paraffin derived from petroleum, coal, or shale oil, thereby being a product of the fossil fuel industry. The wick is made of cotton, a fiber from a plant that requires not only a significant amount of water but also high levels

> **Given how many artisans, shops, and websites cater to our varied aesthetics, it's fairly easy to find multiple appealing options for any tool you're looking for. Unfortunately, this can come at a high price in terms of both human rights and the environment.**

of pesticides and herbicides, after which it is often harvested by child and/or slave labor. The materials were shipped to a factory in China, where the workers may have been subject to sweatshop conditions. The finished candle was wrapped in disposable petroleum-based plastic film and then sent overseas on a cargo ship burning immense amounts of fossil fuels as well as leaving ballast and other water pollution in its wake. The bargain price on the candle at the big-box store is achieved in part by paying employees minimum wage or not much more.

And that's the origin of just one candle. Take the time to trace the origin of the steel in your athame, the glass in your chalice, or the chemical dyes in your altar cloth, and you'll soon begin to see the trails of destruction behind these sacred items. Granted, these same harmful practices taint many things in our lives, everything from smartphones and computers to much of the food we eat. It can feel overwhelming sometimes trying to be a more ethical consumer!

Ethical Options

The trick, of course, is to focus on individual choices rather than trying to change everything at once. Ritual tools are not essential in the same way food or shelter or medicine are. You can practice Paganism without a single physical tool. This means that you have the luxury of taking your time to find something that fits both your ethics and your budget. There are a few potential options for those who want to be more mindful in their purchases but may not have time to fall down the rabbit hole of researching every material and every manufacturer associated with a given item.

As an artist who creates ritual tools, I have a bit of an advantage in that I can make a lot of my tools myself. But I also know how much work goes into creating something by hand, and not everyone has the ability or resources to be able to create a ceramic pentacle or a bone-handled boline. If you choose to buy tools from an artist, you will

almost certainly be paying more than you would at a big-box store, which can put these out of financial reach for some.

You might also have luck finding at least some of your ritual tools outdoors. My wand is a piece of eastern red cedar wood from a fallen tree that I collected well over two decades ago. The handle for my sacred drum is a deer leg bone I found during an important initiation. But I was fortunate enough to have access to open outdoor spaces and the luck to happen across these treasures. Not everyone may have that option.

This is where secondhand tools are a fabulous option. Buying something that has already been in circulation for a while reduces the demand for new materials and new manufacturing. It also helps to keep perfectly good stuff out of the landfills and incinerators. And secondhand things in general are almost always cheaper than brand-new ones, making them budget-friendly, too. Best of all, you never know what you're going to find, so instead of looking at shelves full of a few of the same things over and over again at a big-box store, you instead have a selection of potentially decades of designs and creators to choose from. Who knows what you'll be surprised and delighted to find?

Secondhand Ritual Tools and Where to Find Them

My personal favorite places to look for secondhand ritual tools are thrift stores. I have a whole circuit of them in my area that I like to visit, and the stock is always changing thanks to ongoing donations from the community. Most of them keep their sections pretty stable rather than moving everything around, so I have certain aisles that I gravitate to first to get the best chance of finding something cool. The prices are also generally very reasonable, and I can feel assured that my "rescues" were kept out of the waste stream. (Even the best thrift stores can't sell every single thing they get.)

Antique shops are another fun place to hunt for treasures. Unlike thrift stores, these are generally stocked by a variety of dealers who rent space at a monthly rate. Prices are usually going to be higher, especially on something that has value among certain collectors or hobbyists, though there are exceptions. The condition and quality of items for sale at antique shops is generally going to be higher than at thrift stores, though there are always exceptions in either direction.

If you're up for more of a chase, yard sales and estate sales are delightfully ephemeral sources of possibilities. You'll have to check local online sites (like Craigslist) as well as your local paper to find out about them in advance, though there's also the fun of driving around residential areas on a weekend morning looking for yard sale signs. The selection at these sales is truly unique, with each one being a potpourri of whatever the household decided to try to get rid of. On the bright side, yard sale prices are generally pretty cheap, though estate sales can be pricier, especially those that include an auction for more valuable items.

If you're up for more of a chase, yard sales and estate sales are delightfully ephemeral sources of possibilities.... The selection at these sales is truly unique, with each one being a potpourri of whatever the household decided to try to get rid of.

Don't feel like going out or not able to drive around from place to place? There are online options as well. eBay is the grandmother of secondhand shopping online, and you can find everything from priceless antiques to "that thing I bought on impulse years ago and don't really need anymore, so let's see if I can get a few bucks for it."

Etsy's vintage section also has some interesting finds now and then, though prices tend to be higher. Craigslist may yield the occasional nifty thing (especially furniture that makes a great altar!), though you'll likely have to leave the house to go retrieve it if the seller doesn't offer delivery even for a fee. And if there are any Facebook groups in your area for selling random stuff, keep your eyes peeled there.

Finally, you might ask within your local community if anyone wants to do a swap meet focused on Pagan-related items. It can be a lot of fun to get people together to look through extra books, ritual tools, and other stuff. And it's a great way to rehome what you no longer use while finding what may be more relevant to you now.

But What About the *Energy*?

Over the years I've spent advocating for secondhand ritual tools, one of the things that pops up a lot is concern that these items have someone else's energy all over them. The idea that somebody else handled this knife or that Tarot deck and imbued it with their own energy makes some people think that no one else can ever use it again. Yet they ignore the energy that brand-new tools have soaked into them through the environmental and human rights abuses inherent in their manufacture, transport, and sale.

Purification is one of the first skills many Pagans learn, and it can be used to cleanse secondhand ritual tools more than adequately.

The thing is, purification is one of the first skills many Pagans learn, and it can be used to cleanse secondhand ritual tools more than adequately. Here's a sample purification ritual you can use whenever you have a new-to-you tool, regardless of its source.

Purification Ritual for Secondhand Tools

First, choose a method of purification. Popular ones include washing the item in rainwater or water that has been imbued with the light of the full moon; passing the item through the smoke of sacred incense; burying the item in the ground or leaving it on a windowsill for a full moon cycle; or, for energy workers, "manually" removing the energy. Not all of these will work for every tool, depending on what it's made of, but you are welcome to use whatever method you prefer. You can even use a combination of more than one!

Go to your ritual space and prepare the purification method. Next, sit with the item and feel its energy. You might get glimpses of its previous life with another person, or the source of its materials (for example, the tree a wooden wand came from). You may even speak with the spirit of the tool about who you are, why it came to you, why you've brought it into your home, and how you might work together. Don't make any assumptions or judgments based on what you see or feel; this is a time to create a new future, not dwell on the past.

Next, start the purification process. For brief methods like incense or water cleansing, this may take only a few moments. For something longer, like a monthlong burial or exposure to the moon's cycle, you will simply start the process and then let it go for its appointed time, completing the ritual when it's done.

As you begin the purification, you can say the following (or create your own words):

I thank you, [name of tool], for joining me here and becoming a part of my spiritual path. I honor where you have come from, and I offer you a fresh start with me. Let this purification carry away anything you don't wish to keep while strengthening the best of what you have learned and gained over time.

Once the purification is done, place the tool on your altar in its appointed place and say:

Welcome, [name of tool], and thank you for sharing this space with me. May what we create be always sacred and agreeable to us both. May we bring about the magic that is most needed and become stronger and better together!

You are welcome to add to this or change it however you like. What's important is that your rite allows you and the tool you've brought into your home to begin a new chapter together, even as you both have your own histories that have brought you to this moment in time.

Even if you aren't able to make every single ritual tool in your kit secondhand, every one that you do acquire has the potential to be just as effective as any shiny new tool. I hope you enjoy the hunt for interesting secondhand finds as much as I do, and I wish you much success in your pursuit for these often overlooked treasures!

Lupa *is a naturalist pagan author and artist in the Pacific Northwest. She is the author of several books on nature-based paganism, including* Nature Spirituality From the Ground Up: Connect with Totems in Your Ecosystem, *and the* Tarot of Bones *deck and book. More about Lupa and her works may be found at http://www.thegreenwolf.com.*

Illustrator: M. Kathryn Thompson

Put That Out!
When to Stop a Spell

Diana Rajchel

You set out to cast a spell. You know your intention, you line up your materials and altar space, and you have the directions to follow. Despite following them to the letter, glass candles explode, oils go spontaneously rancid, offerings rot. You realize, once again, that spells aren't recipes. But you aren't sure what happened or what to do about it.

Sometimes you can spot the logical reason for the strange event right away: the glass got too hot, the weather was humid, someone in your house mistook the food offering dish for a charcuterie. Other times, however, strange things happen because Spirit is telling you to stop.

Why Spells Go Wrong

If something strange happens during the "magick in motion" phase of casting a spell, look first for logical explanations. As you do so, refer heavily to the laws of thermodynamics. Glass candleholders break when a flame gets too hot. Hot weather can cause food to go bad. You may have a cat. Move on to the following steps after you rule out all sensible explanations.

When you consider spirit-based possibilities, look first for simple explanations. Examine your intention when you set the spell, and think about your intended result. Most spells fail because of a badly phrased intention or a conflict between the intention and the desired result, or because another entity's desire conflicts with what you want to do.

When we set forth our goals and intentions, we sometimes block each other, usually by accident. Conscious clashes happen because of perceived competition for resources, but often enough it's just because someone expects you to abide by their worldview. We witches can certainly be busybodies!

Warning Signs

By learning the warning signs that a spell has a problem, you can then decide to abandon it or start over. While the list of warning signs here isn't exhaustive, these are the most common signs that a spell isn't performing as intended.

A Bad Feeling

Intuitions flash and get ignored and explained away by practitioners much too often. Emotions, even negative ones, communicate to us what we most need to know. Listen to them, especially during a period of spellwork. If you experience an overwhelming sense of foreboding or loss, stop your spell, partake in cleansing and protection, and perform divination to determine when and if to try again.

Inflammatory Candles

Candles are a popular tool of witchcraft for many reasons, and one of the best advantages they offer is a way to see how your spell is doing right away without having to pull out divination tools. Through us reading their flames, wax melt, and smoke, candles practically talk. When something dramatic happens with them, it's unmissable.

On one occasion, a good-quality candle I prepared looked and felt fine. When I lit it, for no reason I could discern, it made a loud ringing noise that made me sick to my stomach. I put it out immediately. Despite the candle burning for under a minute, the distinctive smell of coal char lingered in the air. I took the hint and threw the candle away after washing it with Florida Water. When a spell needs to stop, candles find a way to let you know. My experiences can veer toward the dramatic. However, fire and flame can give much more subtle "stop" signals than what I typically get.

How Candles Yell, "Stop!"

- On jar candles, char covers the entire glass, with no light spots, even after a day of burning.

- Black smoke

- Hissing and spitting noises

- Sparks jumping from the candle to burn nearby objects
  (Put that out!)

- Flickering and going out, despite multiple relighting attempts,
  with no detectable draft

Candles pose some danger even in the best of circumstances, so pay attention to how they behave while burning. Their unpredictability is why I always place them in large buckets surrounded by water if I must burn one continuously. Even then, a safe burn is not guaranteed. Never leave a burning candle unattended!

When Tarot Cards Smack You

If you are familiar with the tarot, you know that when the Tower card appears in regard to a working, it means "stop." In other divination systems, if you get anything that refers to "stuck" energies, lightning strikes, angered spirits, excessive pain, or ruined relationships with people important to you, take apart your spell. The warnings least heeded involve love magick. People become so fixated on their beloved that they ignore warnings, thinking they can overcome the resistance. Take the hint.

Color Changes

If you build an altar and notice that a fixed object such as a statue suddenly appears shadowy in direct light, that's concerning. Again, always rule out practical explanations first, like dimming light bulbs, but if something suddenly emanates gray, pause. For people who receive psychic perceptions through color, graying signals decay.

Rejected Offerings

In my practice, if a food or drink offering is accepted, it dries/evaporates. If rejected, the food rots. Pay attention, especially if the food rots overnight during dry and cold weather conditions.

Broken Stones

When a stone cracks in half for no discernible reason, take note. Mini cataclysms happen when crystals absorb too much discordant energy. If you happen to be wearing that stone, it may have taken a "hit" for you. For example, if you carry a tiger's-eye for financial insight and the stone cracks, you may find out that your spell has to fight massive market forces and insider trading. If a stone you wear for protection breaks, it warded you from something. Should that happen, bury the broken rock and, if appropriate, start again with a fresh one.

Objects Falling Over and Altars Collapsing

A friend of mine preferred working with forceful spirits, such as daemons. When they didn't like something my friend did, the altar to these spirits collapsed. It did not matter what surface it sat on; if they disapproved, every single item on the altar fell over. Tipsiness can get dangerous if you have candles or breakables on your altar. I have had glass jar candles set in a bowl in the middle of a table tip over despite no floor vibrations at all. When I cleaned up anything unbalancing them and reset the candle, they tipped over again. Items falling over or collapsing indicate that either a spirit you work with disapproves or someone is attempting to suppress your working.

Nightmares

If you experience nightmares more than one night in a row after starting your spell, perform divination or meditate to determine the dream meaning. Attempt to rule out any mundane explanations first: rule out life stress, past trauma, or eating something questionable before bed. If you have a nightmare that focuses on the spell itself, Spirit wants attention pronto.

In most cases, if a spell is somehow generating bad energy, it won't work. On other occasions, it will work in a way that you would probably rather it not. Usually, when the latter happens, you get the results you sought, but you won't like them. For example, you'll draw that new romantic partner—and that's when you find out you've entangled yourself with an obsessive, violent felon. You might get that additional cash you need right now, but then a tax bill arrives and ends up costing you more in the long run. Humans have become short-term thinkers, but the spirit world sees only the long view. Spells and their consequences/results can go on long after an issue no longer has our attention.

> As you establish your intentions, be clear not just about the result but also about how you want to feel at the end. Emotional tone is key to a spell's success.

Spells don't happen in laboratory conditions. Because of that, you can't produce consistent results with them, not in a way that modern science can measure. What you can do is set your intentions with great clarity. As you establish your intentions, be clear not just about the result but also about how you want to feel at the end. Emotional tone is key to a spell's success.

Monitoring a Spell's Performance

Use the following monitors to keep track of a spell's performance. Think of them as the carbon monoxide detectors of magickal practice. Select a method that differs from the elemental alignment of the main spellcasting. For example, if you use candles as your spell, use a vinegar jar as the monitor, and so on. If you are including multiple components for a strong working, you may need to rely on meditation to check in on your spell condition and progress.

Monitor 1: The Vinegar Jar

Put 1 tablespoon sea salt, 1 teaspoon alum crystal, and a blue stone in a clear Mason jar. Fill it half with white vinegar and half with water. Set this on the altar that holds your working, with the lid off. If salt gathers on the jar within a week of you starting your working, stop the spell. Something is interfering enough that the vinegar is neutralizing it. When salt crystallizes at the top of the jar, it signals a pileup of bad energy

Monitor 2: The Tealight

Set a tealight (or miniature glass jar candle) next to your working altar, or, if you carry the spell with you, light the mini candle as part of your daily practice. When you do, think about your spell from a place of curiosity. If the candle burns with black smoke or the glass darkens, perform divination to see if you need to take apart your spell components and start over.

Monitor 3: Inner Vision

Close your eyes and imagine the spell in your mind's eye. Pretend that everything you see behind the spell is nothing more than a stage set. See the stage backdrop lift like a screen to show you what's behind it. You might see a tangle of threads, find an atmospheric sense of anger, or see something else specific and possibly confusing. If you see something especially alarming or sadness-inducing, stop the spell.

Also Valid: Staying the Course

You can let a spell run its course despite warnings. If you choose this, the most likely outcome is that the spell simply won't work. If the results become disruptive, you still have options to change course.

First, you can break any spell that you cast. You may say out loud, "I renounce the spell I cast to _____ (purpose of spell)." If you prefer working with physical material, powdered baker's ammonia breaks spells with great efficiency. Brush a pinch of it on the spell items, and all the spiritual cords connected to the object will break.

If you employed spirits to do the work for you, it might take a little more. If the spirits refuse to quit, you may have to escalate your "stop!" To do this, place a white or black candle on top of a black mirror. Allow the candle to burn safely, with the intention that it vacuum up any energy sent. After the candle finishes burning, cover the mirror for twenty-four hours to avoid removing anything you want to remain. If you raised the energy solely from your own body, recall it with a magnet or lodestone. Take the magnet and hold it in front of your belly button. Tell it to recall all of your spells. Place a second crystal or eucalyptus leaf in your belly button to act as a cleansing filter. Hold the stone, and perform the recall until you feel every bit of what you sent out return to you. You can also set a reversal candle (traditionally a black and red jar candle).

Reset and Redo the Work

As you now recognize, spells are not recipes. You can follow directions to the letter and have the whole thing fall apart with the slightest ill-crafted intention. What spells are is up for debate. Assume each one forms an intelligence that communicates with you, especially when you are on the wrong course. To correct that, learn to admit to yourself when something isn't working. Then you have to make a decision: see the spell through and deal with the consequences inherent in pouring energy that's going wrong into something you want to go right, or stop the spell, cut the energy, and divine what went wrong. The right thing to do depends on your unique situation. Whatever you do, choose wisely.

Diana Rajchel *began her career planning to serve as clergy and write about all subjects spiritual. It did not occur to her or anyone else to say with what agency she might assume priesthood. The result of this oversight in intention setting is that she is now an itinerant city priestess, well-practiced witch, and somewhat unintentional subversive. Her background includes Wicca, folk witchcraft, Conjure, and a whole lot of experience organizing people who don't like knowing that they're organized. Diana splits her time between San Francisco, where she co-owns Golden Apple Metaphysical, and southwestern Michigan, where she runs Earth and Sun spiritual coaching with her partner. Diana has twenty-five years' experience as a professional tarot reader and Western herbalist and twenty-nine years' experience as a professional writer. She is also the pet DragonCat to a very ladylike Boxer named Nora.*

Illustrator: Tim Foley

Envisioning the Future: Practical Tips & Tricks for Vision Board Magic

Michelle Skye

I sit on the floor, listening to the wind play among the trees through the open window. The sun dapples golden streaks and rectangles all around me, warming my feet and the top of my head. All is quiet, save the wind and the laughter of joyous children. I can almost hear the bell of the mobile ice cream truck two streets over, near the barking dog with the blue collar. The scent of fresh-cut grass wafts through the window, and I can feel the stress of modern life drip off me, releasing from my neck and shoulders and jaw. Around me, in a half-circle reminiscent of an earthbound rainbow, I have strewn pictures of various shapes and sizes. Nearby, there is a pair of silver scissors and several glue sticks, the kind that smear on purple but dry clear. There are words, too, and a few treasures I have found: a twisted stick that looks like a bird foot, a piece of blue sea glass, a pearlescent button. Thus begins my vision board practice.

The first time I ever created a vision board, I was with a group of crafty witches in the darkness of an autumn night. Someone had suggested it, and another person came up with a list of necessary items to bring: a medium to large poster board, pictures of things we wished to manifest, words of positivity and abundance, glue, scissors, tiny stones and crystals, and ribbons. We gathered together, in our witchy way, laughing and conversing and sharing food and drink and good company. I don't remember the magic of that evening. I only remember the warm feelings of friendship and connection and community. We all shared our treasures, so there was a little bit of each one of us on our vision boards.

Later that night, we all bundled into our cars as the wind howled and the inky-black branches reached up toward the moon. But later on, as the year progressed, each one of us found our vision board wishes manifested in our lives: a new boyfriend (who turned into a husband), a remodeled bathroom, a healthy outlook on life, and healing. It was amazing! I was officially hooked on the magic of vision boards.

What Is a Vision Board?

A vision board is a representation of what you wish to manifest in your life, as expressed in pictures and color. While words can be added to a vision board, they are not the prominent feature. Traditionally, vision boards were created using paper and glue. While thinking of their dreams and hopes, the crafter would gather pictures from

magazines that represented those goals. These days, pictures found on computers and phones and printed at home are an easier, less time-consuming way to find the perfect image. Once the images are located, they are cut out and pasted onto a poster board in an order that means something to the magical crafter.

That's it! Easy, right? Absolutely—which is part of the power of the vision board. It accesses some element of our past that reminds us of our childhood. Cutting and pasting are skills taught by elementary school teachers to teach fine motor skills to children. You may not remember learning those lessons, but your subconscious does. Way back in the recesses of your brain, the relaxation of cutting and pasting rests next to the joy of coloring. The activity brings with it muscle memory, connected to a time of less responsibility, when you had the opportunity to play outside on a tire swing and run around yelling "tag!" at twilight.

By harnessing the feeling of being a little more free, a little less stifled by the dictates of society, the activity of creating a vision board connects you to your younger self. In some magical traditions, it is this younger self that has the quickest and easiest pathway to the Divine and is the best conduit for magic. Why wouldn't it be? As children, we believe in the possibility of the fantastic. Magic closets, talking animals, and shoes that dance on their own are all a part of our reality. They are real, as real as the ground under our feet or the air singing in our ears as we swing free of gravity.

Tip: If you are a more modern spellcaster and the idea of physical crafting is onerous, never fear! You can still create a vision board—online! The concept is the same, except instead of creating a physical vision board, you create a digital one. For the younger generation, this may actually be as calming as cutting and pasting, as their elementary school lessons often centered around basic computer skills.

There are numerous websites that offer digital vision boards (for a fee), or you can create visual layouts of your goals and wishes on Pinterest for free. You may choose to create an aesthetic or a mood board by using a picture-editing app such as PicsArt. With any of these digital choices, your actions will be the same as with a traditional vision board: you focus on your goal, find visual images that represent that wish or dream, and then arrange the images into a visually pleasing montage. The magic is in the finding of the images and the design of a beautiful, cohesive piece of art that represents your dream.

Another modern option, and one that I often use at work, is to save pictures in a vision board folder and then use them to create a slideshow as the computer background. I have the images on my computer rotate every minute, so I see different pictures fairly frequently, thus reinforcing the subliminal message of striving for my goals. The nice thing about a slideshow background is that you can arrange the pictures in a specific order, just like you would on a poster board. You might choose to have the pictures flow according to color, style, or image type. By determining the order of the pictures on your slideshow, you are energetically connecting yourself to them and to the manifestation of those dreams.

But What's My Dream?

I think the hardest part of creating a vision board is deciding what you actually want to manifest. I can't even tell you how many times I've decided to make a vision board but couldn't, because I didn't know what I wanted! It can be difficult to verbalize what you want in your life. After all, there are so many choices and so many aspects of life to take into consideration.

In my experience, I have found that there are two different ways to approach this roadblock: by planning or by allowing. Both methods are excellent and will help you focus your vision board magic. The method that works best for you really depends on your personality and the way you traditionally direct your life.

Planning

As the word suggests, this pathway is for the person who enjoys making a plan and sticking to it. Not interested in a lot of surprises, the planner likes to be really hands-on with their decision-making. If you are a person who likes to watch travel shows and read travel books before going on vacation, strategizes about where you'll spend your money, and uses a list for birthday and holiday shopping, then planning ahead will probably be the most comfortable and powerful way to identify your goals and create your vision board.

As a planner myself, my suggestion, when starting on your vision board creation, is to focus on one or two main external areas of your life and then one or two internal healing goals. Most recently, I created a vision board at Beltane. I had been struggling to coalesce my life dreams into a workable vision board for months, and I was having trouble figuring out where to even begin. Enter COVID-19. Unfortunately, I was forced to postpone my wedding. I wanted to bring some positivity into my life concerning the postponement, so I took a look at the details of the original planned event that I wanted to alter, even if slightly, and I decided on two things: (1) I wanted to get married outside, preferably in the woods, and (2) I wanted to honeymoon in Egypt. These two major external hopes became the focus of my Beltane vision board.

I then considered what other parts of my life were a concern for me. Obviously, with the upheaval in the world, I wanted to feel grounded and centered. I also wanted to concentrate on self-love and self-acceptance as the next phase in my healing process. I then symbolized these two general wishes for myself with pictures that represented chakra balancing, Mother Earth, the elements, animals, and goddesses. Hearts, quotes to remember to love myself, and pictures of things that bring me joy rounded out my collection of pictures for my vision board. I was ready to begin!

Allowing

Allowing is the other pathway that can help you focus your vision board and decide what dreams you want to manifest. People who enjoy the allowing process are typically those who like surprises. They will travel to a foreign country without a plan and not bother to read about it beforehand. Because they are interested in their immediate experience, allowing gives them the freedom to flow with the moment and be comfortable with their environment. If you are a person who likes to get in your car and drive randomly to see where you end up, finds amazing deals wherever you go, and embraces whatever shows up in your life, then the allowing pathway will probably be the most powerful way for you to manifest your goals through a vision board.

People who enjoy the allowing process are typically those who like surprises.... Because they are interested in their immediate experience, allowing gives them the freedom to flow with the moment and be comfortable with their environment.

My suggestion is to begin by gathering many different pictures that call to you. They don't have to make sense or form a pattern; the only requirement is that you like them. Often, the best way to do this is by collecting magazines you like and just flipping through the pages while listening to your favorite jam. Try not to put a ton of pressure on yourself to find the "perfect" picture. Stay open to the guidance of the universe and cut out the pictures that resonate with you at that moment and time. You can do this while on the internet as well. Look up one phrase, like "elemental goddess" or "Dia de los Muertos," and allow yourself to go wherever the pictures lead you—from elemental goddess to water, to water snake, to Japan, to kitsune, to foxes, to red hair, to Ireland, to Brigid, etc. In this way, you are putting aside your conscious mind and giving your subconscious mind space to direct you. Before you know it, voilà! You will have a pile of pictures ready to be put on your vision board masterpiece.

Creating Your Manifesting Masterpiece

It's important to take a look at the shape you wish to use for your vision board. You can choose any shape you want—circle, square, rectangle, triangle—but each will add a different energy to your creation. They are all powerful in their own way! Choose the shape that connects the most to your own personality, to how you're feeling at the moment, or to your goals and dreams. Here are some ideas:

Square/Rectangle: Stability, order, equality, the four elements

Diamond: Unconventionality, a new perspective, value, "bling"

Circle: Soft, free-flowing, interconnected, feminine

Spiral: Movement, continuity, universality

Triangle: Creativity, the trinity (feminine or masculine), the human form

Of course, you can choose an even more unconventional shape for your board, such as a goddess shape, a tree, a flower, a chalice, a star, etc. The possibilities are endless. Once you've decided on the shape of your vision board, it's time to choose the layout. Once again, that is entirely up to you. The first time I made a vision board (with my witchy friends on that chilly autumn evening), I followed a format that was similar to the Chinese feng shui *bagua*, or energy map (see illustration). It divides the foundation of your vision board into nine sections that correspond to different areas of life. Each section of the bagua is filled with images, colors, and words that correspond to you and that specific area of your life. This method a great way to express gratitude while at the same time reaching for your next goal.

Wealth & Prosperity "Gratitude"	Fame & Reputation "Integrity"	Love & Marriage "Receptivity"
REAR LEFT	REAR MIDDLE	REAR RIGHT
<u>Wood</u>	<u>Fire</u>	<u>Earth</u>
Blues, purple, reds	Reds	Reds, pinks, whites
Health & Family "Strength"	CENTER	Creativity & Children "Joy"
MIDDLE LEFT	<u>Earth</u>	MIDDLE RIGHT
<u>Wood</u>	Yellow, earth tones	<u>Metal</u>
Blues, greens		White, pastels
Knowledge & Self-Cultivation "Stillness"	Career "Depth"	Helpful People & Travel "Synchronicity"
FRONT LEFT	FRONT MIDDLE	FRONT RIGHT
<u>Earth</u>	<u>Water</u>	<u>Metal</u>
Black, blues, greens	Black, dark tones	White, gray, black

As a magical practitioner, another option would be to divide your vision board into quarters that represent the four elements or the four directions. This design template has the added benefit of accessing elemental and directional energy as you place your pictures in each quarter. You can utilize traditional elemental colors, as well as representations, to add additional depth. For instance, if you wish to purchase an expensive piece of home exercise equipment, you might choose to put those pictures in the fire quarter to symbolize your sweat when you work out. Or you could easily place them in the north for connection to the earth, your physical body, and the meeting of material needs. In fact, you could place different images that represent the same goal in different quarters to create a unifying, holistic dream. A variation of this pattern would be an eightfold design, emulating the Wheel of the Year and the eight sabbats.

If you have two main goals that you wish to focus on, try dividing your vision board in half. One side will focus on one goal and the other side will focus on the other goal. If you utilize this pattern, it's a good idea to create connecting images so the

Another option would be to divide your vision board into quarters that represent the four elements or the four directions. This design template has the added benefit of accessing elemental and directional energy as you place your pictures in each quarter. You can utilize traditional elemental colors, as well as representations, to add additional depth.

energy is not divisive or conflicting. The idea of a vision board is to create something beautiful that you enjoy looking at and that will nudge you (and the universe) toward the manifesting of your goals. Contradiction and contention stop the flow of energy toward manifestation, as they build walls and obstacles in order to protect themselves or be "right." Vision boards access the power of the universe to aid you in manifesting your goals. You want to get rid of any walls and deterrents to success, not craft more.

For my Beltane vision board, I used a quarter format and a half format together in a diamond shape. I decorated one half of the diamond with images of forest weddings and the other half with pictures of couples on vacation in Egypt. In the corners, I placed four goddesses who are deeply connected to animal spirits to represent the elements and directions. In the center, I placed a picture of Mother Earth to symbolize my commitment to the environment and to express my gratitude for her sustaining presence in my life. Throughout all four quarters and on both sides of the paper, I sprinkled pictures and words of self-love and affirmation, along with hearts, lots of blue images that called to me, and symbols of centering, such as chakras and labyrinths. These served to make the image a more cohesive whole, reminding me that I am more than just the parts of my life. They helped me to remember that I am a unique and whole individual in the universe.

. . . .

Vision boards are universal. They can be crafted singly or with a group. People of every age can create a vision board, and the magic is accessible to everyone, not just to the Pagan community. There is nothing scary about vision boards. (They have even been used as a plot point in at least two different Hallmark movies!) At the heart of this magic is the innocence of youth and the simple pleasure of finding beautiful pictures, cutting them out, and pasting them on a piece of paper as the sun shines or while sharing food and drink with a group of friends. It is simple magic, yet it is also profound.

I have found great satisfaction in the creation of my vision boards, as well as in looking at them throughout the year. When the cycle has passed and you return to the same time the following year, it is rewarding to see what has transpired and to make note of what didn't materialize in order to direct your vision board design for the next year. Vision boards are magic. They are a conduit of universal power. They aid us in manifesting our dreams and are fun to make. For me, they are the perfect magical craft!

Michelle Skye *is a dedicated tree-hugging, magic-wielding, goddess-loving Pagan. While she is best known for her three goddess books,* Goddess Alive!, Goddess Afoot!, *and* Goddess Aloud!, *she also works closely with many gods and male magic practitioners. Michelle is fond of reading (a lot!), rainbows, crows, oracle decks, walks in the woods, Middle Eastern dance, spellwork, grunge music, silver jewelry (especially if it's sparkly), and quirky '80s movies. She creates crafts and spells with her magic circle, the Crafty Witches, and celebrates the sabbats with her family coven at home. She has been spinning magic into the world her whole life but has been following the Pagan path for just over twenty years.*

Illustrator: Rik Olson

Family Spellcraft

Estha McNevin

Coven and family members are maybe the few people we might trust enough to learn lifelong magick with. How our own family teaches prayer and spellcraft is a kind of talent we pick up just by watching. When we apply these natural methods of Spirit speak and tarot, we have access to our very best guide for spellcraft, because it can lead us to mystically driven family life experiences and help us understand our own spiritual realizations. We are never alone along that journey of perfect love and perfect trust. Nevertheless, when we ask Spirit to enter

into that family ritual space that we share together, a profound and ancient type of familial spellcraft can manifest.

It never ceases to amaze me that the stories and lessons we observe as Pagans are everywhere around us. Tarot is perhaps our greatest cultural asset, and I see it as an essential family-bonding tool because it is the bedrock upon which all Western esoteric culture is built. It unifies us, as humans of a shared planet, in every way. This profound marriage of art and science is the core text of the occult, and it serves the world quite literally as a pocket-size guide to life, death, and resurrection.

Vulnerability and the Meaning of Life

To be mystically vulnerable takes practice. Exercising spiritual trust requires an ability to develop, and then rely on, our own innate instinct. From the shaman to the sorcerer, there are many ways Paganism has made a science of spellcraft as an esoteric art. Tarot within a modern context, rooted in decks like the Rider-Waite and the Thoth Tarot, is an essential key for all spellwork in our temple, Opus Aima Obscurae, because our work is based in Hermetic and Hellenistic magic. In this allegorical way, tarot is a Pagan pictorial bible, and it visually teaches us how to recognize life patterns. Parents in our community treat the cards like a family calling card of love, support, or even reprimand. If you learn the cards together, then kids know what adults are thinking or feeling just by the tarot card that is left out on the family altar.

Spellcraft using the cards often depicts potentialities we will face in life or reveals things we have to overcome. Like a game of poker, cards can be grouped or arranged to depict our situation. Symbolic insight is a surprise: it can show us a map of what's to come in visions, and many decks are designed to awaken psychic skills and connect humanity for the sake of our survival.

Artists and psychologists alike group the images, seemingly to benefit our willing suspension of disbelief. And, just like movies or the myths they depict, it is the images on the cards that seem to stick effortlessly in our mind's eye. We are able to recall some tarot cards with near-perfect detail after only a few minutes of study. These images are a representative guide for our brain. When we use tarot as a code for spellcasting, we are soliciting the planetary and astrological spirits depicted on these cards in deeply philosophical and Pagan expressions of animistic prayer, adapting our spellcraft to what is needed.

In our temple, we always use color and card to set the holy day mood, ritual tone, or elemental roll call of an event. Folks who study color know that using it as a therapy or mental focal aid can be rewarding and healing. We subtly apply colors to family clothing choices, from hunter orange to save a life and spot a kid on the day the Sun card is on the altar to gifting purple scarves to elders on outing days when the Moon card is drawn. Casting color magick as a family is fun because it has always proved a creative and effective family bonding model.

Talking about tarot cards or telling stories that relate them to our lives is a fun part of Pagan family time. Teaching kids to intuit the symbols and understand the images is as easy as describing the card and then asking them what they think is being depicted: what story is each card telling us?

With this in mind, the advice we offer parents is to assign parts of the tarot to each relative age group of the family, so that every member has a way to deepen their astrological knowledge and use our Pagan liturgy in daily living. Talking about tarot cards or telling stories that relate them to our lives is a fun part of Pagan family time. Teaching kids to intuit the symbols and understand the images is as easy as describing the card and then asking them what they think is being depicted: what story is each card telling us?

When cards reflect our elders and community leaders with Atu cards, or trumps, it is sometimes in more ways than we might like. Regal in their own right, parents are always planning the lives of those around them, and socially they are often working to save face, like so many of the personalities we see depicted in the court cards. Children, the ones whom we find to be worth all of the work, for our ambitious love of them, are the pips of the minor arcana, elementally suited in cumulative order from ace to ten. All at once fragile and natural, phenomenally numeric in nature, family spellcraft can be modeled this way to achieve profound results by encouraging all ages to understand the value of shared magick.

The astrological timing expressed in the degrees of each sign creates an endless amount of astronomy-based spellwork, from meteor showers to retrograde cycles, so learning about constellations while casting family spells with tarot cards often requires us to learn a bit of Latin or French as well as colors and numbers to better understand the occult sciences. Opus Aima Obscurae was forged to be an Eastern Hellenistic Pagan temple in part because this is the cultural proclivity of matriarchal polymaths; we craft spells to understand the wisdom of the moment with our children because decoding life for them is a gift.

Family Spell Sets

Here is a quick guide to get you started using the tarot more frequently to determine routine, reward, or adventure. Find your own ways to use the cards on family altars. Weaving them into bedtime stories and pillow spells will help children feel heard and protected when they express an emotional or spiritual need. This guide gives each age group in the family a portion of the deck to draw from and apply to everything from family magick to mealtimes movie or game choices.

ATU CARDS (TRUMPS): ELDERS SEEDING LIFE LESSONS

Colors: White, purple, blue, black
Influence: Wisdom, truth telling, memory sharing
Spellwork: "Why don't we …"

On each of the 22 trump cards of a tarot deck, write a destination or local adventure that is possible to manifest. Try to match the alignments as best you can. For example, on the Star card (Trump XVII) you might write "Planetarium" as an adventure option. The best thing about this sort of magick is that it teaches tarot alignments through experiences and can be literal or figurative. For example, you could, as a family, visit a local planetarium for an astronomical event viewing, or you could just as easily use lights and science to create a map of the stars on the ceiling and learn the constellations together.

The goal for elders in casting family magick is often to share experience and research that has evolved from knowledge into wisdom based on many years of shared magickal experiences. This makes our elders our most valuable resources for crafting new memories. Casting spellwork with them also keeps elders feeling valued and engaged in life.

Elders know things, even the ones who have messed up quite badly, and this is why they so often are a trusted reference point for family magick. Our parents and grandparents are the ones who truly plant the seeds of success or failure in us. When they teach us about the trump cards of the tarot and use them to cast magick, they

> **Our parents and grandparents are the ones who truly plant the seeds of success or failure in us. When they teach us about the trump cards of the tarot and use them to cast magick, they guide our lessons in life.**

guide our lessons in life. In doing so, they inevitably equip us with direct knowledge of the code of creation, enabling us to make more informed choices that can profoundly shape our lives and the world for the better.

Pips: Children Growing Together

Colors: Khaki, green, yellow, cream
Influence: Creatively choosing and cataloging family magick
Spellwork: Family protection, flow and energy work

Children can be better than adults at sensing planetary and daily energy. Not every screaming fit or bad choice is sheer rebellion; some kids simply need to feel that they understand the world and are listened to by adults. Pips are numbers with great scientific significance, and teaching kids to take solace in maths and sacred geometry is what the tarot is designed for. When kids are free to cast their own magick and are given the numerological tools necessary to understand the most rudimentary code of humanity, they feel empowered and inspired, and they share that curiosity and joy with everyone in the family.

Pip-craft is related to goal setting, and the tarot guides us to always set elemental goals. The cycle of the decad is an original evolution of maths. The number 10 and its midpoint 5 have a magical foundation in the principles of Pythagorean maths. Both numbers feature strongly in the origins of European fraternal magic as well as ritual circle-casting and pentagram use in ceremony. Teaching children how to understand and master numbers is a point of pride for most Pagan parents.

The very foundations of the spells we craft and cast today are derived from ancestors who lived so closely in tune with the earth and the rhythms of the universe that the most sustainable and utopian among them have left their contributions to the tarot as a guide. The planet they entrusted us with was not quite so industrialized or filled with an impending sense of global peril that kids sense today.

Giving them an idea of numeric cycles and hidden meanings that express regeneration and eternity truly helps them to shape solutions that we are incapable of ourselves.

Kids should always be empowered with choices and learn how to set their own goals so that they have a truly vested interest in the outcome. Anyone who wants to learn to control their emotions can be tasked to pull all of the cups cards and use them to show us how they feel. We can describe the suit to them and show them how the water travels like our emotions from one vessel to the next, teaching them to control their emotions as they come to understand the story of the cups.

Relating the pips to their feelings by asking how many there are, in what scene they are placed, and so on, helps anyone confused by the power of their feelings to understand better and express them more calmly. In talking together, it becomes easy for them to see how the concept of water is a fluid allegory of emotion that expands from the ace, contracts around the five, and expands again to the tenth increment.

Kids should always be empowered with choices and learn how to set their own goals so that they have a truly vested interest in the outcome. Anyone who wants to learn to control their emotions can be tasked to pull all of the cups cards and use them to show us how they feel.

This rhythm of accumulation between the one, the five, and the ten is repeated in maths as a looping numeric principle. This eternal cycle of fulfillment, in the case of the cups, depicts what we must experience to understand emotional fulfillment.

COURT CARDS: PARENTS FLOWERING CONSCIOUSNESS

Colors: Pink, red, blue, orange
Influence: Daily planetary awareness and planning
Spellwork: Surprises

Using all of the court cards (face cards) from a tarot deck, assign each one a surprise or treat as a way of teaching children the types of luck and manifestation that exist in the Pagan world based on the archetypes of the cards. Knowing the personalities of the face cards helps us to better understand other people and to know the ways that we can surprise or delight them. For example, to surprise the Queen of Coins might require an earthly display of personal savings, so drawing her on the kitchen altar might entail blessing and counting piggy banks or achieving household chores in exchange for an allowance. A special batch of ginger butterbeer from the Queen of Cups or surprises the family can enjoy together, like a new game, might be the rewards that the Queen of Wands offers if everyone works as a team to rake the yard.

Surprises build stronger memories and break the monotony of routine. Adults are often obsessed with routine, so finding witchy ways to delight and dazzle outside of the norm can be a fun and engaging reason to fill the bathtub with water balloons or serve rainbow pancakes for no other apparent reason than sparkles! Whimsy is exactly what it takes for routine to feel desired upon a safe return from adventure.

Finding ways to surprise the entire family and keep a spark of adventure alive is a worthy goal for anyone working to keep others supported and healthy. Moments of sheer astonishment and joy become worth the effort. For example, every autumn I fill the entryway and temple with leaves. It creates a mess and we have to all work together to clean it up, but for a few minutes after our Samhain rituals we get to experience the outside inside and play in the leaves in the library or on the stairs. The ensuing chaos and maddening joy is never a disappointment.

Adults are amazing at planning things and using their busy energy to achieve order and routine. The moments when they are present are an act of love, and surprises keep kids and elders feeling rewarded for continued effort and daily and weekly goals. For example, having kids draw a court card with a surprise written on it is a fun way of treating them when they have achieved a milestone or academic goal. The King of Wands may surprise them with sports equipment, or the King of Cups might reward an act of sibling kindness with a hug and a cup of cocoa. Creating new rewards for courtly services is a fun way to encourage kids to notice what needs to be done around the house and pitch in.

. . . .

Use these ideas as inspiration to come up with your own fun ways to use the tarot as a family to teach and understand Pagan values.

Estha McNevin (*Missoula, MT*) *is a Priestess and Eastern Hellenistic oracle of Opus Aima Obscuræ, a nonprofit matriarchal Pagan temple haus. Since 2003 she has dedicated her life to working as a ceremonialist, psychic, lecturer, freelance author, and artist. In addition to hosting public sabbats, Estha organizes annual philanthropic projects, teaches classes, counsels clients, manages the temple farm, conducts ceremonies, and officiates for the temple divination rituals each dark moon. To learn more, please explore www.opusaimaobscurae.org and www.facebook.com/opusaimaobscurae.*

Illustrator: M. Kathryn Thompson

Ways to Work with the Full Moon

Najah Lightfoot

During the time of the Full Moon, there are many ways to proceed as a magickal, spiritual person.

Lunar madness. Witchy workings. Full moons. Eclipses. The number 13. Waxing cycle of power culminating in a powerful time to cast spells, say prayers, or set intentions.

High magick. Low magick. No magick.

Draw a pentagram. Cast a circle, or simply light a candle and blow a kiss. Write poetry, paint, color in a magickal coloring book, write songs, or plant a magickal herb or plant according to the time of year.

Start a dream journal. Watch a scary movie. Listen to haunting melodies. (One of my favorite tunes is "Lullaby" by Nox Arcana. It's so dreamy and mystical.)

Sit on your porch and gaze at the sky, or perhaps choose to arise in the middle of the night and go outside.

All these things are available for you to do, or not, during the time of the Full Moon.

The Full Moon always calls to me, whether I intentionally intend to "keep it" or not. What I mean by "keep it" is to perform a ritual specifically on the nights of the Full Moon: the night before, the night of, or the night after.

I used to spend a lot of time planning what to do for the Full Moon. I would consult my magickal datebooks and make plans for an elaborate circle or casting. Sometimes, if the fates allowed, I'd be blessed to gather with other Witches or like-minded people to practice our rites.

These days, not so much. I'm mainly a solitary Witch now. I always have been, for the most part, and it seems that destiny likes me being that way, despite my many attempts to change that status. During the time of COVID-19, the global pandemic, I was glad I had a lot of practice being on my own.

It's not that I haven't tried to join a coven or group. One of my most memorable Full Moons was when a group of spectacular Witches allowed me to keep the Full Moon with them while I was on a business trip in New Orleans. I will never forget their kindness and hospitality. But I live in Colorado, and I can't just hop on my broom and fly to New Orleans every Full Moon, as much as I'd like to!

So the Moon and I are pretty much left on our own, but it always seems to work out.

I'll go to bed not realizing it's one of the nights of the Full Moon, only to be awakened by a power greater than myself, a force beyond my being, and be drawn to the window. There she'll be, shining bright in all her glory, lighting up my bedroom.

If the nighttime doesn't call to me, I'll awaken early in the morning before sunrise, and as I ascend the steps to my back door, there she'll be, round and bright in the western sky. When I see the Full Moon in her supernatural state, I feel like I can reach out and touch her. Not wanting to waste this precious moment, I'll grab my candles and incense, go outside, and say a heartfelt prayer.

Lunar Madness

Lately, I'll have a breakdown, some type of emotional crying jag, a venting upheaval of emotions that leaves me drained and shaken. Then, after the explosion has occurred, I'll look at my calendar and see it's the time of the Full Moon! Even if I do try to get ahead of it, she always trips me up somehow. But I'm working on it. I've started highlighting on my calendar a full week before the Full Moon occurs, calling it my "Full Moon zone," so I can be better prepared to work with my emotions. I may not schedule events or appointments during this time, depending on the people or the situation. At some point in our lives, we have to accept ourselves as we are and give ourselves a break.

Dates, Times, and Cycles

We keep time by the Moon. Our monthly calendar is derived from the number of days it takes the Moon to complete one cycle, from New Moon to New Moon. The word *lunacy* stems from the root word *lunar*, which means "Moon." Lunacy refers to an intermittent type of insanity associated with the Moon. Would it be safe to say a lunatic is someone who is utterly senseless during the time of the Full Moon, but the rest of the time is completely sane? Hmm. It does give one pause.

Folklore is full of anecdotal lunar references. Dogs howl at the Moon, healthcare workers know a Full Moon means an increase in emergency services, and sailors pay attention to the Moon, for it is a scientific fact that the Moon controls the tides and exerts a gravitational pull on the Earth.

Certain animals spawn during the Full Moon. And if you've been blessed to see the moonlight upon a water's surface, well, that's a magickal experience indeed.

So how can we as magickal, spiritual people work with the Full Moon? How can we harness some of its power for our workings?

Magickal Moon Rites and Workings

We can keep our lunar rites simple or we can make them complex. It depends on our intention and whether we are doing the rite as a solitary Witch or with a group or coven.

Solitary rites are deeply personal, for there is no one around but you. One my favorite things to do at the Full Moon is to take a witchy bath or shower. I like to light candles, pour fragrant essential oils into the bathwater, bathe with luxurious soaps, and escape into my own little world of magick. After my bath, I often put on a flowing robe and settle in with one of my favorite movies, and when the time is right, I light a candle in my pentagram candleholder, say my prayers, and blow a kiss to the Moon.

Covens or groups may plan elaborate rites, with each person performing a specific task for the night's workings. People may assume different personas. One person may act as

One my favorite things to do at the Full Moon is to take a witchy bath or shower. I like to light candles, pour fragrant essential oils into the bathwater, bathe with luxurious soaps, and escape into my own little world of magick.

the High Priestess or Priest, and another may carry the censer. Someone may be responsible for water and libations. Others may recite poetry or dance. You can do all of these things on your own, but it's a lot of work. I know this from experience!

In Closing

How you choose to honor the Full Moon is up to you. The Moon doesn't need us; it is we who need her. Let her breathe vision into your dreams and rites.

Be easy on yourself, especially in times of stress. Go with the flow of your days and nights. Remember the Moon, honor her, and bless her. In the end, you may discover new ways to expand yourself as a magickal, spiritual, witchy person!

Najah Lightfoot *is the multi-award-winning author of* Good Juju: Mojos, Rites & Practices for the Magical Soul. *She is the Gold Medal winner of the 2020 COVR Awards in the category of Wicca, Witchcraft, and Magick, and a winner of the 2019 NYC Big Book Award. She is a fellow of the Sojourner Truth Leadership Circle, sponsored by Auburn Seminary. Najah practices magick, loves rituals, and enjoys writing about ways to help others develop powerful spiritual, magickal practices. She resides in Denver, Colorado, where the blue skies and the power of the Rocky Mountains uplift and fill her soul. She is also an initiated member of a New Orleans Vodou society and a regular contributing author to the Llewellyn annuals. Najah is a frequent guest on podcasts, as well as an in-demand speaker for conferences, classes, and events, and her beloved magickal staff is now on display at the Buckland Museum of Witchcraft & Magick in Cleveland, Ohio. Najah can be found online @NajahLightfoot on Twitter, Instagram, and Facebook.*

Illustrator: Tim Foley

How to Use the Craft to Make the Decision to Retire

Emyme

Retirement. Almost every worker experiences this milestone eventually. After over five decades of being part of the great American workforce, I recently (finally) made the decision to voluntarily leave the world of full-time employment. As I approach my mid-sixties, the thought of having more time in the day to devote to my health, my family, my writing, and my Craft grew from an idea sometime in the future to a goal with a hard deadline. The pandemic of 2020 shifted that deadline several times, which was inconvenient and frightening but also served as the push I needed to choose a firm date and stick to it.

Years ago, when I first began thinking about retirement, age and health were the prominent deciding factors. For decades it had been my dream to retire from full-time work at age fifty-eight, while I was still young and healthy enough to enjoy volunteering, writing, travel, and perhaps a part-time job. Several circumstances eventually made that unrealistic, so I committed to work until my full retirement age. Family situations influenced the decision. I found myself sharing a home with my elderly mother, and several years later I became a grandmother. (This moved me into the first level of the crone stage of life.) The next two factors that came into play were income and workplace issues. Over and above any well-earned government assistance a person might receive in retirement, savings and investments are required to live without a guaranteed paycheck; however, difficult and stressful workplace issues may decrease the value of a paycheck.

It is my nature to be a lazy procrastinator, and I prefer to make decisions after consulting others' opinions and doing some research. Therefore I called upon my earth-based beliefs to assist me in making the decision to retire. As I examined the factors involved, it occurred to me that the four elements aligned with four considerations:

- **WATER = Age and Health:** Water is necessary for life; there is no survival without it. It may be a constant flow, moving forward, like age, or it may be stagnant, like poor health.

- **EARTH = Family:** Whoever makes up your family, they are a foundation beneath your feet, steady and firm, holding you up as the earth does, grounding you.

- **AIR = Income:** Air flow may be just enough, a perfect breeze, or it may be nonexistent or blowing too hard. Air changes direction.

- **FIRE = Current Workplace Issues:** It is a rare workplace that has no fires to be extinguished. Some flare-ups can be beneficial, like the burning of deadwood to keep other trees healthy, while other times a complete burning of bridges is required.

Water

Water is needed to live. The years move constantly onward, like water does. If we are lucky enough to live to an old age, at various times we may say our life has flooded, flowed, or slowed to a trickle. Likewise, our health will ebb and flow. Sometimes, unfortunately, our health may become more like a stagnant pool. Poor health due to illness or a less-than-fit lifestyle may leave us treading water even as age keeps flowing by. My age had streamed on while my health ebbed and flowed and was somewhat sluggish. I took action, stirring the pool with a stick, breaking down the dam, to release the water. This came in the form of more mundane, less magickal actions such as making appointments with various health professionals, followed by scheduling important tests and necessary procedures. Setting a retirement date was the dead-line I needed to achieve my fitness goals and increase the flow of my age stream. (Acquiring adequate health care coverage now that I am no longer part of an employer plan is a work in progress.)

Earth

A solid foundation is vital for support through life events. Family may be your immediate biological members or those less closely related to you, or it may be your family of choice, such as those with the same belief system, social media groups, neighbors, and people you know through clubs and avocations. For the past fifteen years, I have shared a home with my mother, my father (since passed), and my daughter (grown and flown). Until recently it was just my mother and me. Now

her age and health issues necessitate her living with another relative, which leaves me with all of the home expenses until I am ready to sell. The process of selling and moving brings another level of activity, akin to a minor earthquake. Sorting through a decade and a half—no, a lifetime—of collected and stored objects, purging the not needed/unwanted, organizing the needed/wanted, cleansing, and then locating my next home has required lots of positive energy. Setting a firm retirement date was what I needed to shift my earth foundation, that slight quake, and move my footing slightly to another support and live closer to my daughter and her family.

Air

Some may deny it, some may say it takes very little, but the reality is that some form of money is necessary to exist anywhere on the globe. Like water, air may be not a constant force. When we're settled in a secure job, money is like a light spring breeze, flowing slowly and steadily. Sometimes there is a burst of energy: blizzards, hurricanes, tornados—whether good (an unexpected windfall, a lottery win, a work bonus) or bad (an unexpected repair, a higher than usual utility bill, a decrease in work hours). Sometimes there is no movement to the air due to a lack of revenue in any form: loss of job, loss of second income. Setting a retirement date motivated me to meet with a financial advisor, pay off debts, increase my savings, and complete the process for obtaining retirement benefits.

Fire

If there is an industry, service, or business, profit or nonprofit, that never has any conflict of any type, I have yet to hear of it. Based on the simple fact that the successful performance of jobs involves people, there will be tension and disputes, with metaphorical fires small, medium, and large needing to be extinguished. Poor communication, changes in management, loss of contracts, and termination of staff all cause stress. But stress is also generated by success and growth, which allows for promotions and requires hiring, movement to larger facilities, and scheduling adjustments. Fire is a force that warms and mesmerizes, yet it harms and destroys when not properly lit and tended. A candle can scent a room; a forest fire can obliterate many homes. A firm retirement date was the deadline I needed to get away from the fires of discord and disruption that arose from personality conflicts and light a fire under the cauldron of my creative writing.

Spirit

While I was accomplishing/starting all of the above, I determined it wise to ask for indications that it was the right time for retirement. My spells for guidance are almost always directed to the universe and/or the Creator/Creatrix. Part of every spell includes a request to clearly see that I am on the right path. For such a life-changing event as retirement, I appealed to nature, especially my spirit animal the chipmunk, and birds. Soon my daily walks had me finding feathers of all sorts, and one day no fewer than twelve types of birds visited the feeders in my backyard, some of which I had not seen in years. Indeed, I knew I was on the right path when a rarely seen favorite—the nuthatch—perched in the garden by my window one day. The wisdom of the nuthatch includes being adept at seeing both sides of an issue and moving from thought to action.

More unmistakable spiritual support came my way via three little messengers. Early one morning, a small frog greeted me in the driveway. A symbol of prosperity and cleansing, frogs clear away the barriers to abundance. In all my years at this home, I had never seen a frog on the property. Returning from a walk, I discovered that a cicada had found its way to the front porch. These noisy jewel-colored insects symbolize transformation, regeneration, and long life. Again, although

I had often heard them, I had never seen a cicada so close to my home. While retrieving the mail one day, a grasshopper stood watch on the mailbox. I admit to having seen many grasshoppers in my yards and gardens, but the timing of this visit seemed particularly providential. I interpreted the appearance of this grasshopper to mean changes were happening, and I must be ready to take advantage of any opportunity presented to me. I needed to make a magnificent jump. I was convinced: retirement was the right course for me.

I interpreted the appearance of this grasshopper to mean changes were happening, and I must be ready to take advantage of any opportunity presented to me. I needed to make a magnificent jump.

The final step was to choose a date. For this I worked with my go-to magic: numbers. The original date was to be a day in January of 2021, but work and family issues forced me to change it to July of 2020. Further work, family, and then world issues compelled me to move the date to late summer of 2021. Throughout the process, I knew I would know the right date for me when I saw it: 5/14/2021 or 8/13/2021 or 9/10/2021? That last date was my final choice. Nine and 10 (September 10 = 9 + 10) add to 19, in the year 2021 (19/2021). The flow of the numbers felt right. I also took into account the dates of Mercury retrograde, making sure to avoid one of those potentially disruptive periods.

For anyone who has ever retired and agonized over when and how to do so—or who has had to make a decision about any issue, for that matter—there must have been a "decider" This is a definitive event that makes you say, "Okay, that's it. This is my choice." What was the eventual "decider" for me? As I mentioned earlier, it was the turmoil and upheaval of the year 2020. It requires no explanation, and any comment on that year would be an entirely new essay, so I will leave it at that.

Sending all good thoughts and positive energy to anyone contemplating the next season of life. Blessed be.

Emyme *resides in southern New Jersey and is currently easing from the autumn of life to winter, and from mother to crone. A solitary eclectic, she especially enjoys researching obscure feast days. Alpha-numeric spells and candle, crystal, kitchen, and hedge magick also play a role in her Craft life. Emyme can be reached at catsmeow24@verizon.net. All is well, life is good, blessed be.*

Illustrator: Bri Hermanson

The Lunar Calendar

September 2021 to December 2022

SEPTEMBER
S	M	T	W	T	F	S
			1	2	3	4
5	6	7	8	9	10	11
12	13	14	15	16	17	18
19	20	21	22	23	24	25
26	27	28	29	30		

OCTOBER
S	M	T	W	T	F	S
					1	2
3	4	5	6	7	8	9
10	11	12	13	14	15	16
17	18	19	20	21	22	23
24	25	26	27	28	29	30
31						

NOVEMBER
S	M	T	W	T	F	S
	1	2	3	4	5	6
7	8	9	10	11	12	13
14	15	16	17	18	19	20
21	22	23	24	25	26	27
28	29	30				

DECEMBER
S	M	T	W	T	F	S
			1	2	3	4
5	6	7	8	9	10	11
12	13	14	15	16	17	18
19	20	21	22	23	24	25
26	27	28	29	30	31	

2022

JANUARY
S	M	T	W	T	F	S
						1
2	3	4	5	6	7	8
9	10	11	12	13	14	15
16	17	18	19	20	21	22
23	24	25	26	27	28	29
30	31					

FEBRUARY
S	M	T	W	T	F	S
		1	2	3	4	5
6	7	8	9	10	11	12
13	14	15	16	17	18	19
20	21	22	23	24	25	26
27	28					

MARCH
S	M	T	W	T	F	S
		1	2	3	4	5
6	7	8	9	10	11	12
13	14	15	16	17	18	19
20	21	22	23	24	25	26
27	28	29	30	31		

APRIL
S	M	T	W	T	F	S
					1	2
3	4	5	6	7	8	9
10	11	12	13	14	15	16
17	18	19	20	21	22	23
24	25	26	27	28	29	30

MAY
S	M	T	W	T	F	S
1	2	3	4	5	6	7
8	9	10	11	12	13	14
15	16	17	18	19	20	21
22	23	24	25	26	27	28
29	30	31				

JUNE
S	M	T	W	T	F	S
			1	2	3	4
5	6	7	8	9	10	11
12	13	14	15	16	17	18
19	20	21	22	23	24	25
26	27	28	29	30		

JULY
S	M	T	W	T	F	S
					1	2
3	4	5	6	7	8	9
10	11	12	13	14	15	16
17	18	19	20	21	22	23
24	25	26	27	28	29	30
31						

AUGUST
S	M	T	W	T	F	S
	1	2	3	4	5	6
7	8	9	10	11	12	13
14	15	16	17	18	19	20
21	22	23	24	25	26	27
28	29	30	31			

SEPTEMBER
S	M	T	W	T	F	S
				1	2	3
4	5	6	7	8	9	10
11	12	13	14	15	16	17
18	19	20	21	22	23	24
25	26	27	28	29	30	

OCTOBER
S	M	T	W	T	F	S
						1
2	3	4	5	6	7	8
9	10	11	12	13	14	15
16	17	18	19	20	21	22
23	24	25	26	27	28	29
30	31					

NOVEMBER
S	M	T	W	T	F	S
		1	2	3	4	5
6	7	8	9	10	11	12
13	14	15	16	17	18	19
20	21	22	23	24	25	26
27	28	29	30			

DECEMBER
S	M	T	W	T	F	S
				1	2	3
4	5	6	7	8	9	10
11	12	13	14	15	16	17
18	19	20	21	22	23	24
25	26	27	28	29	30	31

SEPTEMBER 2021

SU	M	T	W
29	30	31	**1** 4th ♊ ☽ → ♋ 1:26 am
5 4th ♌ ☽ v/c 10:22 am ☽ → ♍ 7:06 pm	**6** 4th ♍ New Moon 8:52 pm ● *New Moon* *Labor Day*	**7** 1st ♍ ☽ v/c 3:24 pm ☽ → ♎ 11:20 pm	**8** 1st ♎
12 1st ♏ ☽ v/c 1:33 am ☽ → ♐ 4:34 am	**13** 1st ♐ 2nd Quarter 4:39 pm ◑	**14** 2nd ♐ ☽ v/c 6:57 am ☽ → ♑ 7:34 am ♂ → ♎ 8:14 pm	**15** 2nd ♑
19 2nd ♓	**20** 2nd ♓ ☽ v/c 7:55 pm Full Moon 7:55 pm ○ ☽ → ♈ 11:13 pm *Harvest Moon*	**21** 3rd ♈	**22** 3rd ♈ ☉ → ♎ 3:21 pm ☽ v/c 10:05 pm *Mabon* *Sun enters Libra* *Fall Equinox*
26 3rd ♊	**27** 3rd ♊ ☿ ℞ 1:10 am *Mercury retrograde*	**28** 3rd ♊ ☽ v/c 12:18 am ☽ → ♋ 9:34 am 4th Quarter 9:57 pm ◑	**29** 4th ♋
3	4	5	6

Eastern Daylight Time (EDT)

ZODIAC SIGNS			PLANETS	
♈ Aries	♌ Leo	♐ Sagittarius	☉ Sun	♃ Jupiter
♉ Taurus	♍ Virgo	♑ Capricorn	☽ Moon	♄ Saturn
♊ Gemini	♎ Libra	♒ Aquarius	☿ Mercury	♅ Uranus
♋ Cancer	♏ Scorpio	♓ Pisces	♀ Venus	♆ Neptune
			♂ Mars	♇ Pluto

TH	F	SA	NOTES
4th ♋ **2**	4th ♋ **3** ☽ v/c 1:37 am ☽ → ♌ 11:58 am	4th ♌ **4**	
1st ♎ **9**	1st ♎ **10** ☽ v/c 12:48 am ☽ → ♏ 2:05 am ♀ → ♏ 4:39 pm	1st ♏ **11**	
2nd ♑ **16** ☽ v/c 1:40 am ☽ → ♒ 11:23 am	2nd ♒ **17**	2nd ♒ **18** ☽ v/c 5:14 am ☽ → ♓ 4:22 pm	
3rd ♈ **23** ☽ → ♉ 8:38 am	3rd ♉ **24**	3rd ♉ **25** ☽ v/c 9:09 am ☽ → ♊ 8:36 pm	
4th ♋ **30** ☽ v/c 10:49 am ☽ → ♌ 8:53 pm	**1**	**2**	
7	**8**	**9**	

ASPECTS & MOON PHASES

☌ Conjunction	0°	● New Moon	(1st Quarter)
✶ Sextile	60°	◑ Waxing Moon	(2nd Quarter)
☐ Square	90°	○ Full Moon	(3rd Quarter)
△ Trine	120°	◐ Waning Moon	(4th Quarter)
⚻ Quincunx	150°		
☍ Opposition	180°		

OCTOBER 2021

SU	M	T	W
26	27	28	29
3 4th ♌ ☽ → ♍ 4:38 am	**4** 4th ♍	**5** 4th ♍ ☽ v/c 4:46 am ☽ → ♎ 8:41 am	**29** ● 4th ♎ New Moon 7:05 am ♇ D 2:29 pm *New Moon*
10 1st ♐ ♄ D 10:17 pm	**11** 1st ♐ ☽ v/c 12:30 am ☽ → ♑ 1:15 pm	**12** 1st ♑ 2nd Quarter 11:25 pm ◑	**13** 2nd ♑ ☽ v/c 6:53 am ☽ → ♒ 4:47 pm
17 2nd ♓ ☽ v/c 7:24 pm	**18** 2nd ♓ ♃ D 1:30 am ☽ → ♈ 6:04 am ☿ D 11:17 am *Mercury direct*	**19** 2nd ♈	**20** ○ 2nd ♈ ☽ v/c 10:57 am Full Moon 10:57 am ☽ → ♉ 3:59 pm *Blood Moon*
24 3rd ♊	**25** 3rd ♊ ☽ v/c 10:11 am ☽ → ♋ 5:00 pm	**26** 3rd ♋	**27** 3rd ♋
31 4th ♍ *Samhain* *Halloween*	**1**	**2**	**3**

Eastern Daylight Time (EDT)

ZODIAC SIGNS

♈ Aries	♌ Leo	♐ Sagittarius
♉ Taurus	♍ Virgo	♑ Capricorn
♊ Gemini	♎ Libra	♒ Aquarius
♋ Cancer	♏ Scorpio	♓ Pisces

PLANETS

☉ Sun	♃ Jupiter
☽ Moon	♄ Saturn
☿ Mercury	♅ Uranus
♀ Venus	♆ Neptune
♂ Mars	♇ Pluto

TH	F	SA	NOTES
30	4th ♌ 1	4th ♌ 2 ☽ v/c 7:43 pm	
1st ♎ 7 ☽ v/c 1:03 am ♀ → ♐ 7:21 am ☽ → ♏ 10:22 am	1st ♏ 8	1st ♏ 9 ☽ v/c 2:05 am ☽ → ♐ 11:24 am	
2nd ♒ 14	2nd ♒ 15 ☽ v/c 8:33 am ☽ → ♓ 10:22 pm	2nd ♓ 16	
3rd ♉ 21	3rd ♉ 22 ☽ v/c 4:35 pm	3rd ♉ 23 ☉ → ♏ 12:51 am ☽ → ♊ 3:57 am *Sun enters Scorpio*	
3rd ♋ ◑ ☽ v/c 2:02 am ☽ → ♌ 5:07 am 4th Quarter 4:05 pm	4th ♌ 29	4th ♌ 30 ☽ v/c 3:05 am ♂ → ♏ 10:21 am ☽ → ♍ 2:09 pm	
4	5	6	

ASPECTS & MOON PHASES

☌	Conjunction	0°	● New Moon	(1st Quarter)
✶	Sextile	60°	◐ Waxing Moon	(2nd Quarter)
□	Square	90°	○ Full Moon	(3rd Quarter)
△	Trine	120°	◑ Waning Moon	(4th Quarter)
⊼	Quincunx	150°		
☍	Opposition	180°		

NOVEMBER 2021

SU	M	T	W
31	**1** 4th ♍ ☽ v/c 1:00 pm ☽ → ♎ 7:11 pm	**2** 4th ♎ *Election Day (general)*	**3** 4th ♎ ☽ v/c 6:32 pm ☽ → ♏ 8:52 pm
7 1st ♐ ☽ v/c 8:44 am ☽ → ♑ 8:03 pm *Daylight Saving Time ends at 2:00 am*	**8** 1st ♑	**9** 1st ♑ ☽ v/c 12:51 pm ☽ → ♒ 10:03 pm	**10** 1st ♒
14 2nd ♓ ☽ v/c 12:40 am ☽ → ♈ 10:48 am	**15** 2nd ♈	**16** 2nd ♈ ☽ v/c 10:51 am ☽ → ♉ 9:18 pm	**17** 2nd ♉
21 3rd ♊ ☽ v/c 10:52 am ☉ → ♐ 9:34 pm ☽ → ♋ 10:33 pm *Sun enters Sagittarius*	**22** 3rd ♋	**23** 3rd ♋	**24** 3rd ♋ ☽ v/c 12:46 am ☿ → ♐ 10:36 am ☽ → ♌ 10:59 am
28 4th ♍ ☽ v/c 7:02 pm	**29** 4th ♍ ☽ → ♎ 3:55 am	**30** 4th ♎ ☽ v/c 11:20 pm	**1**
5	**6**	**7**	**8**

Eastern Daylight Time (EDT) becomes Eastern Standard Time (EST) November 7

NOVEMBER 2021

TH	F	SA	NOTES
4th ♏ New Moon 5:15 pm ●	1st ♏ 5 ♀ → ♑ 6:44 am ☽ v/c 12:10 pm ☿ → ♏ 6:35 pm ☽ → ♐ 8:52 pm	1st ♐ 6	
New Moon			
1st ♒ ◑ 2nd Quarter 7:46 am ☽ v/c 2:52 pm	2nd ♒ 12 ☽ → ♓ 2:54 am	2nd ♓ 13	
2nd ♉ 18	2nd ♉ ○ ☽ v/c 3:57 am Full Moon 3:57 am ☽ → ♊ 9:33 am *Mourning Moon* *Lunar Eclipse*	3rd ♊ 20	
3rd ♌ 25	3rd ♌ 26 ☽ v/c 11:24 am ☽ → ♍ 9:12 pm	3rd ♍ ◑ 4th Quarter 7:28 am	
Thanksgiving Day			
2	3	4	
9	10	11	

DECEMBER 2021

SU	M	T	W
28	29	30	1 4th ♎ ☽ → ♏ 6:55 am Ψ D 8:22 am
5 1st ♐ ☽ v/c 12:08 am ☽ → ♑ 6:31 am	6 1st ♑ ☽ v/c 11:42 pm	7 1st ♑ ☽ → ♒ 6:49 am	8 1st ♒
12 2nd ♈	13 2nd ♈ ♂ → ♐ 4:53 am ☿ → ♑ 12:52 pm ☽ v/c 9:52 pm	14 2nd ♈ ☽ → ♉ 3:11 am	15 2nd ♉
19 3rd ♊ ☽ v/c 1:02 am ☽ → ♋ 4:42 am ♀ ℞ 5:36 am	20 3rd ♋	21 3rd ♋ ☽ v/c 9:44 am ☉ → ♑ 10:59 am ☽ → ♌ 4:54 pm *Yule* *Sun enters Capricorn* *Winter Solstice*	22 3rd ♌
26 3rd ♍ ☽ v/c 3:39 am ☽ → ♎ 11:24 am 4th Quarter 9:24 pm ◑	27 4th ♎	28 4th ♎ ☽ v/c 4:11 pm ☽ → ♏ 4:16 pm ♃ → ♓ 11:09 pm	29 4th ♏
2	3	4	5

Eastern Standard Time (EST)

ZODIAC SIGNS

♈ Aries	♌ Leo	♐ Sagittarius
♉ Taurus	♍ Virgo	♑ Capricorn
♊ Gemini	♎ Libra	♒ Aquarius
♋ Cancer	♏ Scorpio	♓ Pisces

PLANETS

☉ Sun	♃ Jupiter
☽ Moon	♄ Saturn
☿ Mercury	♅ Uranus
♀ Venus	♆ Neptune
♂ Mars	♇ Pluto

DECEMBER 2021

TH	F	SA	NOTES
4th ♏ **2**	4th ♏ **3** ☽ v/c 12:22 am ☽ → ♐ 7:13 am	4th ♐ ● New Moon 2:43 am *New Moon* *Solar Eclipse*	
1st ♒ **9** ☽ v/c 5:00 am ☽ → ♓ 9:53 am	1st ♓ ◑ 2nd Quarter 8:36 pm	2nd ♓ **11** ☽ v/c 2:40 pm ☽ → ♈ 4:46 pm	
2nd ♉ **16** ☽ v/c 11:08 am ☽ → ♊ 3:43 pm	2nd ♊ **17**	2nd ♊ ○ Full Moon 11:36 pm *Long Nights Moon*	
3rd ♌ **23**	3rd ♌ **24** ☽ v/c 1:39 am ☽ → ♍ 3:24 am *Christmas Eve*	3rd ♍ **25** *Christmas Day*	
4th ♏ **30** ☽ v/c 12:10 pm ☽ → ♐ 6:08 pm	4th ♐ **31** *New Year's Eve*	I	
6	7	8	

JANUARY 2022

SU	M	T	W
26	27	28	29
2 ● 4th ♑ ☿ → ≈ 2:10 am New Moon 1:33 pm *New Moon*	**3** 1st ♑ ☽ v/c 11:21 am ☽ → ≈ 5:44 pm	**4** 1st ≈ ☽ v/c 7:45 pm	**5** 1st ≈ ☽ → ♓ 7:17 pm
9 ◐ 1st ♈ 2nd Quarter 1:11 pm	**10** 2nd ♈ ☽ v/c 2:23 am ☽ → ♉ 9:47 am	**11** 2nd ♉	**12** 2nd ♉ ☽ v/c 2:39 pm ☽ → ♊ 10:08 pm
16 2nd ♋	**17** ○ 2nd ♋ ☽ v/c 6:48 pm Full Moon 6:48 pm ☽ → ♌ 11:03 pm *Martin Luther King Jr. Day* *Cold Moon*	**18** 3rd ♌ ♅ D 10:27 am	**19** 3rd ♌ ☉ → ≈ 9:39 pm *Sun enters Aquarius*
23 3rd ♎	**24** 3rd ♎ ♂ → ♑ 7:53 am ☽ v/c 5:10 pm ☽ → ♏ 10:57 pm	**25** ◑ 3rd ♏ 4th Quarter 8:41 am ☿ → ♑ 10:05 pm	**26** 4th ♏
30 4th ♑ ☽ v/c 11:44 pm	**31** 4th ♑ ☽ → ≈ 4:43 am	I	2

Eastern Standard Time (EST)

ZODIAC SIGNS

♈ Aries	♌ Leo	♐ Sagittarius
♉ Taurus	♍ Virgo	♑ Capricorn
♊ Gemini	♎ Libra	≈ Aquarius
♋ Cancer	♏ Scorpio	♓ Pisces

PLANETS

☉ Sun	♃ Jupiter
☽ Moon	♄ Saturn
☿ Mercury	♅ Uranus
♀ Venus	♆ Neptune
♂ Mars	♇ Pluto

JANUARY 2022

TH	F	SA	NOTES
30	31	**1** 4th ♐ ☽ v/c 3:16 am ☽ → ♑ 6:02 pm *New Year's Day*	
6 1st ♓	**7** 1st ♓ ☽ v/c 5:23 pm	**8** 1st ♓ ☽ → ♈ 12:26 am	
13 2nd ♊	**14** 2nd ♊ ☿ R 6:41 am ☽ v/c 9:22 pm *Mercury retrograde*	**15** 2nd ♊ ☽ → ⊗ 11:11 am	
20 3rd ♌ ☽ v/c 3:15 am ☽ → ♍ 9:02 am	**21** 3rd ♍	**22** 3rd ♍ ☽ v/c 2:46 pm ☽ → ♎ 5:03 pm	
27 4th ♏ ☽ v/c 12:28 am ☽ → ♐ 2:34 am	**28** 4th ♐ ☽ v/c 2:00 pm	**29** 4th ♐ ♀ D 3:46 am ☽ → ♑ 4:09 am *Venus direct*	
3	4	5	

Aspects & Moon Phases

☌ Conjunction	0°	● New Moon	(1st Quarter)
✳ Sextile	60°	◑ Waxing Moon	(2nd Quarter)
□ Square	90°	○ Full Moon	(3rd Quarter)
△ Trine	120°	◐ Waning Moon	(4th Quarter)
⊼ Quincunx	150°		
☍ Opposition	180°		

FEBRUARY 2022

SU	M	T	W
30	**31**	**2** ♈ 4th ≈ New Moon 12:46 am ● ☽ v/c 6:01 am *Lunar New Year (Tiger)* *New Moon*	**2** 1st ≈ ☽ → ♓ 6:00 am *Imbolc* *Groundhog Day*
6 1st ♈ ☽ v/c 12:21 pm ☽ → ♉ 5:52 pm	**7** 1st ♉	**8** 1st ♉ 2nd Quarter 8:50 am ◑ ☽ v/c 11:48 pm	**9** 2nd ♉ ☽ → ♊ 5:27 am
13 2nd ♋	**14** 2nd ♋ ☽ v/c 5:27 am ☽ → ♌ 6:17 am ☿ → ≈ 4:54 pm *Valentine's Day*	**15** 2nd ♌	**16** 2nd ♌ ☽ v/c 11:56 am Full Moon 11:56 am ○ ☽ → ♍ 3:42 pm *Quickening Moon*
20 3rd ♎	**21** 3rd ♎ ☽ v/c 12:02 am ☽ → ♏ 4:19 am *Presidents' Day*	**22** 3rd ♏	**23** 3rd ♏ ☽ v/c 4:24 am ☽ → ♐ 8:29 am 4th Quarter 5:32 pm ◑
27 4th ♑ ☽ v/c 9:49 am ☽ → ≈ 1:36 pm	**28** 4th ≈ ☽ v/c 9:01 pm	**1**	**2**
6	**7**	**8**	**9**

Eastern Standard Time (EST)

FEBRUARY 2022

TH	F	SA	NOTES
1st ♓ ☿ D 11:13 pm **3** *Mercury direct*	1st ♓ **4** ☽ v/c 4:41 am ☽ → ♈ 9:57 am	1st ♈ **5**	
2nd ♊ **10**	2nd ♊ **11** ☽ v/c 3:23 am ☽ → ♋ 6:27 pm	2nd ♋ **12**	
3rd ♍ **17**	3rd ♍ **18** ☉ → ♓ 11:43 am ☽ v/c 6:20 pm ☽ → ♎ 10:51 pm *Sun enters Pisces*	3rd ♎ **19**	
4th ♐ **24** ☽ v/c 10:24 pm	4th ♐ **25** ☽ → ♑ 11:27 am	4th ♑ **26**	
3	**4**	**5**	
10	**11**	**12**	

Aspects & Moon Phases

☌ Conjunction	0°	● New Moon	(1st Quarter)
✶ Sextile	60°	◗ Waxing Moon	(2nd Quarter)
☐ Square	90°	○ Full Moon	(3rd Quarter)
△ Trine	120°	◖ Waning Moon	(4th Quarter)
⊼ Quincunx	150°		
☍ Opposition	180°		

MARCH 2022

SU	M	T	W
27	28	**1** 4th ≈ ☽ → ♓ 3:53 pm *Mardi Gras (Fat Tuesday)*	**2** 4th ♓ New Moon 12:35 pm ● *New Moon* *Ash Wednesday*
6 1st ♈ ♂ → ≈ 1:23 am ♀ → ≈ 1:30 am ☽ → ♉ 3:00 am	**7** 1st ♉	**8** 1st ♉ ☽ v/c 9:35 am ☽ → ♊ 1:40 pm	**9** 1st ♊ ☿ → ♓ 8:32 pm
13 2nd ♋ EDT in effect 2:00 am ☽ v/c 11:44 am ☽ → ♌ 3:32 pm *Daylight Saving Time* *begins at 2:00 am*	**14** 2nd ♌	**15** 2nd ♌ ☽ v/c 6:56 am	**16** 2nd ♌ ☽ → ♍ 12:59 am
20 3rd ♎ ☽ v/c 8:40 am ☉ → ♈ 11:33 am ☽ → ♏ 11:45 am *Ostara* *Sun enters Aries* *Spring Equinox*	**21** 3rd ♏	**22** 3rd ♏ ☽ v/c 12:01 pm ☽ → ♐ 2:59 pm	**23** 3rd ♐
27 4th ≈ ☿ → ♈ 3:44 am	**28** 4th ≈ ☽ v/c 10:11 am	**29** 4th ≈ ☽ → ♓ 12:32 am	**30** 4th ♓
3	4	5	6

Eastern Standard Time (EST) becomes Eastern Daylight Time (EDT) March 13

ZODIAC SIGNS

♈ Aries	♌ Leo	♐ Sagittarius
♉ Taurus	♍ Virgo	♑ Capricorn
♊ Gemini	♎ Libra	≈ Aquarius
♋ Cancer	♏ Scorpio	♓ Pisces

PLANETS

☉ Sun	♃ Jupiter
☽ Moon	♄ Saturn
☿ Mercury	♅ Uranus
♀ Venus	♆ Neptune
♂ Mars	♇ Pluto

MARCH 2022

TH	F	SA	NOTES
3 1st ♓ ☽ v/c 4:45 pm ☽ → ♈ 7:52 pm	**4** 1st ♈	**5** 1st ♈ ☽ v/c 11:02 pm	
11 ◑ 1st ♊ 2nd Quarter 5:45 am ☽ v/c 11:43 am	**11** 2nd ♊ ☽ → ♋ 2:24 am	**12** 2nd ♋	
17 2nd ♍ *St. Patrick's Day*	**18** ○ 2nd ♍ Full Moon 3:18 am ☽ v/c 4:11 am ☽ → ♎ 7:26 am *Storm Moon*	**19** 3rd ♎	
24 3rd ♐ ☽ v/c 8:59 am ☽ → ♑ 5:54 pm	**25** ◑ 3rd ♑ 4th Quarter 1:37 am	**26** 4th ♑ ☽ v/c 7:51 pm ☽ → ♒ 8:55 pm	
31 4th ♓ ☽ v/c 2:37 am ☽ → ♈ 5:30 am	*1*	*2*	
7	*8*	*9*	

Aspects & Moon Phases

☌ Conjunction	0°	● New Moon	(1st Quarter)
⚹ Sextile	60°	◐ Waxing Moon	(2nd Quarter)
☐ Square	90°	○ Full Moon	(3rd Quarter)
△ Trine	120°	◑ Waning Moon	(4th Quarter)
⚻ Quincunx	150°		
☍ Opposition	180°		

APRIL 2022

SU	M	T	W
27	28	29	30
3 1st ♉	**4** 1st ♉ ☽ v/c 9:53 pm ☽ → ♊ 11:04 pm	**5** 1st ♊ ♀ → ♓ 11:18 am	**6** 1st ♊ ☽ v/c 11:15 pm
10 2nd ♌ ☽ → ♌ 12:00 am ☿ → ♉ 10:09 pm	**11** 2nd ♌	**12** 2nd ♌ ☽ v/c 6:16 am ☽ → ♍ 10:07 am	**13** 2nd ♍
17 3rd ♏ *Easter*	**18** 3rd ♏ ☽ v/c 7:55 pm ☽ → ♐ 10:16 pm	**19** 3rd ♐ ☉ → ♉ 10:24 pm *Sun enters Taurus*	**20** 3rd ♐ ☽ v/c 4:56 pm ☽ → ♑ 11:52 pm
24 4th ♒ ☽ v/c 8:33 pm	**25** 4th ♒ ☽ → ♓ 6:15 am	**26** 4th ♓	**27** 4th ♓ ☽ v/c 9:36 am ☽ → ♈ 12:10 pm
1	2	3	4

Eastern Daylight Time (EDT)

ZODIAC SIGNS

♈ Aries	♌ Leo	♐ Sagittarius
♉ Taurus	♍ Virgo	♑ Capricorn
♊ Gemini	♎ Libra	♒ Aquarius
♋ Cancer	♏ Scorpio	♓ Pisces

PLANETS

☉ Sun	♃ Jupiter
☽ Moon	♄ Saturn
☿ Mercury	♅ Uranus
♀ Venus	♆ Neptune
♂ Mars	♇ Pluto

APRIL 2022

TH	F	SA	NOTES
31	**4th ♈** New Moon 2:24 am ● *All Fools' Day* *New Moon*	**1st ♈ 2** ☽ v/c 9:51 am ☽ → ♉ 12:50 pm	
1st Ⅱ 7 ☽ → ♋ 11:30 am	**1st ♋ 8**	**1st ♋** ◑ 2nd Quarter 2:48 am ☽ v/c 9:01 pm	
2nd ♍ 14 ☽ v/c 2:11 pm ☽ → ♎ 4:46 pm ♂ → ♓ 11:06 pm	**2nd ♎ 15** *Good Friday*	**2nd ♎** ○ Full Moon 2:55 pm ☽ v/c 5:57 pm ☽ → ♏ 8:23 pm *Wind Moon*	
3rd ♑ 21	**3rd ♑ 22** ☽ v/c 11:53 pm *Earth Day*	**3rd ♑** ◑ ☽ → ♒ 2:17 am 4th Quarter 7:56 am	
4th ♈ 28	**4th ♈ 29** ♀ ℞ 2:38 pm ☽ v/c 5:38 pm ☿ → Ⅱ 6:23 pm ☽ → ♉ 8:19 pm	**4th ♉** ● New Moon 4:28 pm *Solar Eclipse/ New Moon*	
5	**6**	**7**	

ASPECTS & MOON PHASES

☌	Conjunction	0°	● New Moon	(1st Quarter)
⚹	Sextile	60°	◑ Waxing Moon	(2nd Quarter)
□	Square	90°	○ Full Moon	(3rd Quarter)
△	Trine	120°	◑ Waning Moon	(4th Quarter)
⚻	Quincunx	150°		
☍	Opposition	180°		

MAY 2022

SU	M	T	W
1 1st ♉ Beltane	**2** 1st ♉ ☽ v/c 6:13 am ☽ → ♊ 6:47 am ♀ → ♈ 12:10 pm	**3** 1st ♊	**4** 1st ♊ ☽ v/c 4:37 pm ☽ → ♋ 7:05 pm
8 1st ♌ 2nd Quarter 8:21 pm ◑ Mother's Day	**9** 2nd ♌ ☽ v/c 8:39 am ☽ → ♍ 6:53 pm	**10** 2nd ♍ ☿ ℞ 7:47 am ♃ → ♈ 7:22 pm Mercury retrograde	**11** 2nd ♍
15 2nd ♏	**16** 2nd ♏ Full Moon 12:14 am ○ ☽ v/c 5:28 am ☽ → ♐ 7:50 am Lunar Eclipse/ Flower Moon	**17** 3rd ♐ ☽ v/c 11:59 pm	**18** 3rd ♐ ☽ → ♑ 8:02 am
22 3rd ♒ ◑ ☽ v/c 3:19 am ☽ → ♓ 11:49 am 4th Quarter 2:43 pm ☿ → ♉ 9:15 pm	**23** 4th ♓	**24** 4th ♓ ☽ v/c 5:33 pm ☽ → ♈ 5:39 pm ♂ → ♈ 7:17 pm	**25** 4th ♈
29 4th ♉ ☽ v/c 10:11 am ☽ → ♊ 1:23 pm	**30** 4th ♊ New Moon 7:30 am ● New Moon Memorial Day	**31** 1st ♊ ☽ v/c 4:10 pm	**1**
5	**6**	**7**	**8**

Eastern Daylight Time (EDT)

ZODIAC SIGNS

♈ Aries	♌ Leo	♐ Sagittarius
♉ Taurus	♍ Virgo	♑ Capricorn
♊ Gemini	♎ Libra	♒ Aquarius
♋ Cancer	♏ Scorpio	♓ Pisces

PLANETS

☉ Sun	♃ Jupiter
☽ Moon	♄ Saturn
☿ Mercury	♅ Uranus
♀ Venus	♆ Neptune
♂ Mars	♇ Pluto

MAY 2022

TH	F	SA	NOTES
1st ⊗ **5**	1st ⊗ **6**	1st ⊗ **7** ☽ v/c 6:26 am ☽ → ♌ 7:50 am	
2nd ♍ **12** ☽ v/c 12:00 am ☽ → ♎ 2:34 am	2nd ♎ **13**	2nd ♎ **14** ☽ v/c 4:07 am ☽ → ♏ 6:34 am	
3rd ♑ **19**	3rd ♑ **20** ☽ v/c 8:00 am ☽ → ♒ 8:53 am ☉ → ♊ 9:23 pm *Sun enters Gemini*	3rd ♒ **21**	
4th ♈ **26** ☽ v/c 11:20 pm	4th ♈ **27** ☽ → ♉ 2:22 am	4th ♉ **28** ♀ → ♉ 10:46 am	
2	**3**	**4**	
9	**10**	**11**	

ASPECTS & MOON PHASES

☌ Conjunction	0°	● New Moon (1st Quarter)
✶ Sextile	60°	◑ Waxing Moon (2nd Quarter)
☐ Square	90°	○ Full Moon (3rd Quarter)
△ Trine	120°	◐ Waning Moon (4th Quarter)
⊼ Quincunx	150°	
☍ Opposition	180°	

JUNE 2022

SU	M	T	W
29	30	31	**1** 1st ♊ ☽ → ♋ 1:49 am
5 1st ♌ ☽ v/c 7:12 pm	**6** 1st ♌ ☽ → ♍ 2:22 am	**7** 1st ♍ 2nd Quarter 10:48 am ◑	**8** 2nd ♍ ☽ v/c 8:09 am ☽ → ♎ 11:23 am
12 2nd ♏ ☽ v/c 5:40 pm ☽ → ♐ 6:31 pm	**13** 2nd ♐ ☿ → ♊ 11:27 am	**14** 2nd ♐ Full Moon 7:52 am ○ ☽ v/c 10:58 am ☽ → ♑ 6:14 pm *Strong Sun Moon*	**15** 3rd ♑
19 3rd ♓ *Father's Day* *Juneteenth*	**20** 3rd ♓ ☽ v/c 11:11 pm ◐ 4th Quarter 11:11 pm ☽ → ♈ 11:37 pm	**21** 4th ♈ ☉ → ♋ 5:14 am *Litha* *Sun enters Cancer* *Summer Solstice*	**22** 4th ♈ ♀ → ♊ 8:34 pm
26 4th ♊	**27** 4th ♊ ☽ v/c 10:38 pm	**28** 4th ♊ ♆ ℞ 3:55 am ● ☽ → ♋ 7:53 am New Moon 10:52 pm *New Moon*	**29** 1st ♋
3	4	5	6

Eastern Daylight Time (EDT)

ZODIAC SIGNS

♈ Aries	♌ Leo	♐ Sagittarius
♉ Taurus	♍ Virgo	♑ Capricorn
♊ Gemini	♎ Libra	♒ Aquarius
♋ Cancer	♏ Scorpio	♓ Pisces

PLANETS

☉ Sun	♃ Jupiter
☽ Moon	♄ Saturn
☿ Mercury	♅ Uranus
♀ Venus	♆ Neptune
♂ Mars	♇ Pluto

JUNE 2022

TH	F	SA	NOTES
1st ⊗ **2**	1st ⊗ **3** ☿ D 4:00 am ☽ v/c 11:15 am ☽ → ♌ 2:38 pm *Mercury direct*	1st ♌ **4** ♄ ℞ 5:47 pm	
2nd ♎ **9**	2nd ♎ **10** ☽ v/c 1:36 pm ☽ → ♏ 4:41 pm	2nd ♏ **11**	
3rd ♑ **16** ☽ v/c 2:41 pm ☽ → ♒ 5:44 pm	3rd ♒ **17**	3rd ♒ **18** ☽ v/c 2:50 pm ☽ → ♓ 7:01 pm	
4th ♈ **23** ☽ v/c 4:02 pm ☽ → ♉ 7:58 am	4th ♉ **24**	4th ♉ **25** ☽ v/c 3:02 pm ☽ → ♊ 7:13 pm	
1st ⊗ **30** ☽ v/c 4:14 pm ☽ → ♌ 8:40 pm	*1*	*2*	
7	*8*	*9*	

JULY 2022

SU	M	T	W
26	27	28	29
3 1st ♌ ☽ v/c 5:59 am ☽ → ♍ 8:31 am	**4** 1st ♍ *Independence Day*	**5** 1st ♍ ♂ → ♉ 2:04 am ☿ → ♋ 2:25 am ☽ v/c 2:04 pm ☽ → ♎ 6:25 pm	**5** 1st ♎ 2nd Quarter 10:14 pm ◑
10 2nd ♏ ☽ v/c 12:34 am ☽ → ♐ 4:34 am	**11** 2nd ♐ ☽ v/c 9:42 pm	**12** 2nd ♐ ☽ → ♑ 5:01 am	**12** 2nd ♑ Full Moon 2:38 pm ○ *Blessing Moon*
17 3rd ♓ ♀ → ♋ 9:32 pm	**18** 3rd ♓ ☽ v/c 2:43 am ☽ → ♈ 7:17 am	**19** 3rd ♈ ☿ → ♌ 8:35 am	**19** 3rd ♈ ☽ v/c 10:19 am 4th Quarter 10:19 am ◑ ☽ → ♉ 2:23 pm
24 4th ♊	**25** 4th ♊ ☽ v/c 4:14 am ☽ → ♋ 1:54 pm	**26** 4th ♋	**27** 4th ♋ ☽ v/c 8:54 pm
31 1st ♍	1	2	3

Eastern Daylight Time (EDT)

ZODIAC SIGNS

♈ Aries	♌ Leo	♐ Sagittarius
♉ Taurus	♍ Virgo	♑ Capricorn
♊ Gemini	♎ Libra	♒ Aquarius
♋ Cancer	♏ Scorpio	♓ Pisces

PLANETS

☉ Sun	♃ Jupiter
☽ Moon	♄ Saturn
☿ Mercury	♅ Uranus
♀ Venus	♆ Neptune
♂ Mars	♇ Pluto

JULY 2022

TH	F	SA	NOTES
30	1st ♌ **1**	1st ♌ **2**	
2nd ♎ **7** ☽ v/c 9:04 pm	2nd ♎ **8** ☽ → ♏ 1:15 am	2nd ♏ **9**	
3rd ♑ **14** ☽ v/c 12:17 am ☽ → ♒ 4:13 am	3rd ♒ **15**	3rd ♒ **16** ☽ v/c 12:36 am ☽ → ♓ 4:18 am	
4th ♉ **21**	4th ♉ **22** ☉ → ♌ 4:07 pm ☽ v/c 7:45 pm *Sun enters Leo*	4th ♉ **23** ☽ → ♊ 1:11 am	
4th ♋ ● **28** ☽ → ♌ 2:36 am New Moon 1:55 pm ♃ ℞ 4:37 pm *New Moon*	1st ♌ **29**	1st ♌ **30** ☽ v/c 12:29 am ☽ → ♍ 2:11 pm	
4	5	6	

Aspects & Moon Phases

☌ Conjunction	0°	● New Moon	(1st Quarter)
✶ Sextile	60°	◗ Waxing Moon	(2nd Quarter)
□ Square	90°	○ Full Moon	(3rd Quarter)
△ Trine	120°	◖ Waning Moon	(4th Quarter)
⊼ Quincunx	150°		
☍ Opposition	180°		

AUGUST 2022

SU	M	T	W
31	**1** 1st ♍ ☽ v/c 6:29 pm *Lammas*	**2** 1st ♍ ☽ → ♎ 12:06 am	**3** 1st ♎
7 2nd ♐	**8** 2nd ♐ ☽ v/c 6:30 am ☽ → ♑ 2:39 pm	**9** 2nd ♑	**10** 2nd ♑ ☽ v/c 12:39 pm ☽ → ♒ 2:45 pm
14 3rd ♓ ☽ v/c 11:11 am ☽ → ♈ 4:43 pm	**15** 3rd ♈	**16** 3rd ♈ ☽ v/c 4:18 pm ☽ → ♉ 10:22 pm	**17** 3rd ♉
21 4th ♊ ☽ v/c 6:06 pm m ☽ → ♋ 8:29 pm	**22** 4th ♋ ☉ → ♍ 11:16 pm *Sun enters Virgo*	**23** 4th ♋	**24** 4th ♋ ☽ v/c 5:40 am ☽ → ♌ 9:09 am ♅ ℞ 9:54 am
28 1st ♍ ☽ v/c 11:08 pm	**29** 1st ♍ ☽ → ♎ 5:45 am	**30** 1st ♎	**31** 1st ♎ ☽ v/c 6:43 am ☽ → ♏ 1:11 pm
4	**5**	**6**	**7**

Eastern Daylight Time (EDT)

ZODIAC SIGNS

♈ Aries   ♌ Leo   ♐ Sagittarius
♉ Taurus   ♍ Virgo   ♑ Capricorn
♊ Gemini   ♎ Libra   ♒ Aquarius
♋ Cancer   ♏ Scorpio   ♓ Pisces

PLANETS

☉ Sun   ♃ Jupiter
☽ Moon   ♄ Saturn
☿ Mercury   ♅ Uranus
♀ Venus   ♆ Neptune
♂ Mars   ♇ Pluto

AUGUST 2022

TH	F	SA	NOTES
1st ♎︎ **4** ☽ v/c 2:20 am ☿ → ♍︎ 2:58 am ☽ → ♏︎ 7:47 am	1st ♏︎ ◑ 2nd Quarter 7:07 am	2nd ♏︎ **6** ☽ v/c 7:24 am ☽ → ♐︎ 12:39 pm	
2nd ♒︎ ○ ♀ → ♌︎ 2:30 pm Full Moon 9:36 pm *Corn Moon*	3rd ♒︎ **12** ☽ v/c 7:07 am ☽ → ♓︎ 2:44 pm	3rd ♓︎ **13**	
3rd ♉︎ **18**	3rd ♉︎ ◑ **19** 4th Quarter 12:36 am ☽ v/c 7:06 am ☽ → ♊︎ 8:06 am	4th ♊︎ **20** ♂ → ♊︎ 3:56 am	
4th ♌︎ **25** ☿ → ♎︎ 9:03 pm ☽ v/c 11:55 pm	4th ♌︎ **26** ☽ → ♍︎ 8:25 pm	4th ♍︎ ● New Moon 4:17 am *New Moon*	
1	**2**	**3**	
8	**9**	**10**	

ASPECTS & MOON PHASES

☌ Conjunction	0°	● New Moon (1st Quarter)
✶ Sextile	60°	◑ Waxing Moon (2nd Quarter)
☐ Square	90°	○ Full Moon (3rd Quarter)
△ Trine	120°	◖ Waning Moon (4th Quarter)
⚻ Quincunx	150°	
☍ Opposition	180°	

SEPTEMBER 2022

SU	M	T	W
28	**29**	**30**	**31**
4 2nd ♐ ☽ v/c 9:51 pm ☽ → ♑ 10:03 pm	**5** 2nd ♑ ♀ → ♍ 12:05 am *Labor Day*	**6** 2nd ♑ ☽ v/c 5:43 pm ☽ → ♒ 11:41 pm	**7** 2nd ♒
11 3rd ♓ ☽ → ♈ 2:47 am	**12** 3rd ♈	**13** 3rd ♈ ☽ v/c 12:53 am ☽ → ♉ 7:39 am	**14** 3rd ♉
18 4th ♊ ☽ → ♋ 3:59 am	**19** 4th ♋	**20** 4th ♋ ☽ v/c 11:57 am ☽ → ♌ 4:38 pm	**21** 4th ♌
26 ● 4th ♍ ☽ v/c 8:49 am ☽ → ♎ 12:43 pm New Moon 5:55 pm *New Moon*	**26** 1st ♎	**27** 1st ♎ ☽ v/c 12:21 pm ☽ → ♏ 7:15 pm	**28** 1st ♏
2	**3**	**4**	**5**

Eastern Daylight Time (EDT)

ZODIAC SIGNS

♈ Aries	♌ Leo	♐ Sagittarius
♉ Taurus	♍ Virgo	♑ Capricorn
♊ Gemini	♎ Libra	♒ Aquarius
♋ Cancer	♏ Scorpio	♓ Pisces

PLANETS

☉ Sun	♃ Jupiter
☽ Moon	♄ Saturn
☿ Mercury	♅ Uranus
♀ Venus	♆ Neptune
♂ Mars	♇ Pluto

SEPTEMBER 2022

TH	F	SA	NOTES
1st ♏︎ **1**	1st ♏︎ **2** ☽ v/c 1:22 pm ☽ → ♐︎ 6:39 pm	1st ♐︎ ◑ 2nd Quarter 2:08 pm	
2nd ♒︎ **8** ☽ v/c 8:34 am	2nd ♒︎ **9** ☽ → ♓︎ 12:42 am ☿ ℞ 11:38 pm *Mercury retrograde*	2nd ♓︎ ○ Full Moon 5:59 am ☽ v/c 8:29 pm *Harvest Moon*	
3rd ♉︎ **15** ☽ v/c 8:59 am ☽ → ♊︎ 4:16 pm	3rd ♊︎ **16**	3rd ♊︎ ◑ ☽ v/c 5:52 pm 4th Quarter 5:52 pm	
4th ♌︎ **22** ☽ v/c 7:07 am ☉ → ♎︎ 9:04 pm *Mabon* *Sun enters Libra* *Fall Equinox*	4th ♌︎ **23** ☽ → ♍︎ 3:53 am ☿ → ♍︎ 8:04 am	4th ♍︎ **24**	
1st ♏︎ **29** ♀ → ♎︎ 3:49 am ☽ v/c 5:20 pm	1st ♏︎ **30** ☽ → ♐︎ 12:03 am	*1*	
6	*7*	*8*	

ASPECTS & MOON PHASES

☌ Conjunction	0°	● New Moon	(1st Quarter)
✶ Sextile	60°	◑ Waxing Moon	(2nd Quarter)
☐ Square	90°	○ Full Moon	(3rd Quarter)
△ Trine	120°	◐ Waning Moon	(4th Quarter)
⊼ Quincunx	150°		
☍ Opposition	180°		

OCTOBER 2022

SU	M	T	W
25	**26**	**27**	**28**
2 1st ♐ ☽ → ♑ 3:38 am ☿ D 5:07 am 2nd Quarter 8:14 pm *Mercury direct* ◑	**3** 2nd ♑ ☽ v/c 11:49 pm	**4** 2nd ♑ ☽ → ♒ 6:20 am	**5** 2nd ♒ ☽ v/c 6:46 pm
9 2nd ♈ Full Moon 4:55 pm *Blood Moon* ○	**10** 3rd ♈ ☽ v/c 10:02 am ☽ → ♉ 5:04 pm ☿ → ♎ 7:51 pm	**11** 3rd ♉	**12** 3rd ♉ ☽ v/c 5:42 pm
16 3rd ♋	**17** 3rd ♋ 4th Quarter 1:15 pm ☽ v/c 4:56 pm ◑	**18** 4th ♋ ☽ → ♌ 12:45 am	**19** 4th ♌
23 4th ♎ ♄ D 12:07 am ♀ → ♏ 3:52 am ☉ → ♏ 6:36 am *Sun enters Scorpio*	**24** 4th ♎ ☽ v/c 8:36 pm	**25** 4th ♎ ☽ → ♏ 3:18 am New Moon 6:49 am *Solar Eclipse/ New Moon* ●	**26** 1st ♏
30 1st ♑ ♂ R 9:26 am *Mars retrograde*	**31** 1st ♑ ☽ v/c 11:14 am ☽ → ♒ 11:43 am *Samhain Halloween*	**1** ♊	**2**

Eastern Daylight Time (EDT)

ZODIAC SIGNS

♈ Aries	♌ Leo	♐ Sagittarius
♉ Taurus	♍ Virgo	♑ Capricorn
♊ Gemini	♎ Libra	♒ Aquarius
♋ Cancer	♏ Scorpio	♓ Pisces

PLANETS

☉ Sun	♃ Jupiter
☽ Moon	♄ Saturn
☿ Mercury	♅ Uranus
♀ Venus	♆ Neptune
♂ Mars	♇ Pluto

OCTOBER 2022

TH	F	SA	NOTES
29	30	1st ♐ ☽ v/c 5:46 pm I	
2nd ≈ 6 ☽ → ♓ 8:47 am	2nd ♓ 7	2nd ♓ 8 ☽ v/c 7:10 am ☽ → ♈ 11:57 am ♀ D 5:56 pm	
3rd ♉ 13 ☽ → ♊ 1:08 am	3rd ♊ 14	3rd ♊ 15 ☽ v/c 12:11 am ☽ → ♋ 12:11 pm	
4th ♌ 20 ☽ v/c 6:35 am ☽ → ♍ 12:25 pm	4th ♍ 21	4th ♍ 22 ☽ v/c 2:17 pm ☽ → ♎ 9:24 pm	
1st ♏ 27 ☽ v/c 12:27 am ☽ → ♐ 6:55 am	1st ♐ 28 ♃ → ♓ 1:10 am	1st ♐ 29 ☽ v/c 9:10 am ☽ → ♑ 9:21 am ☿ → ♏ 3:22 pm	
3	4	5	

Aspects & Moon Phases

☌ Conjunction	0°	● New Moon	(1st Quarter)
⚹ Sextile	60°	◗ Waxing Moon	(2nd Quarter)
▢ Square	90°	○ Full Moon	(3rd Quarter)
△ Trine	120°	◗ Waning Moon	(4th Quarter)
⚻ Quincunx	150°		
☍ Opposition	180°		

NOVEMBER 2022

SU	M	T	W
30	31	**1st ≈** 2nd Quarter 2:37 am ◑	**2nd ≈** 2 ☽ v/c 7:08 am ☽ → ♓ 2:46 pm
2nd ♈ 6 EST in effect 2:00 am ☽ v/c 5:30 pm *Daylight Saving Time ends at 2:00 am*	**2nd ♈** 7 ☽ → ♉ 12:15 am	**2nd ♉** ○ Full Moon 6:02 am *Lunar Eclipse/ Mourning Moon Election Day (general)*	**3rd ♉** 9 ☽ v/c 7:00 am ☽ → ♊ 8:37 am
3rd ♋ 13	**3rd ♋** 14 ☽ v/c 5:41 am ☽ → ♌ 7:48 am	**3rd ♌** 15	**3rd ♌** ◑ ♀ → ♐ 1:09 am 4th Quarter 8:27 am ☽ v/c 6:55 pm ☽ → ♍ 8:04 pm
4th ♎ 20	**4th ♎** 21 ☽ v/c 6:14 am ☽ → ♏ 12:16 pm	**4th ♏** 22 ☉ → ♐ 3:20 am *Sun enters Sagittarius*	**4th ♏** ● ☽ v/c 1:16 pm ☽ → ♐ 3:16 pm New Moon 5:57 pm ♃ D 6:02 pm *New Moon*
1st ♑ 27 ☽ v/c 3:11 pm ☽ → ≈ 5:07 pm	**1st ≈** 28	**1st ≈** 29 ☽ v/c 1:53 am ☽ → ♓ 7:15 pm	**1st ♓** ◑ 2nd Quarter 9:37 am
4	5	6	7

Eastern Daylight Time (EDT) becomes Eastern Standard Time (EST) November 6

ZODIAC SIGNS

♈ Aries	♌ Leo	♐ Sagittarius
♉ Taurus	♍ Virgo	♑ Capricorn
♊ Gemini	♎ Libra	≈ Aquarius
♋ Cancer	♏ Scorpio	♓ Pisces

PLANETS

☉ Sun	♃ Jupiter
☽ Moon	♄ Saturn
☿ Mercury	♅ Uranus
♀ Venus	♆ Neptune
♂ Mars	♇ Pluto

NOVEMBER 2022

TH	F	SA	NOTES
3 2nd ♓	**4** 2nd ♓ ☽ v/c 6:05 pm ☽ → ♈ 7:07 pm	**5** 2nd ♈	
10 3rd ♊	**11** 3rd ♊ ☽ v/c 5:28 pm ☽ → ♋ 7:22 pm *Veterans Day*	**12** 3rd ♋	
17 4th ♍ ☿ → ♐ 3:42 am	**18** 4th ♍	**19** 4th ♍ ☽ v/c 3:47 am ☽ → ♎ 5:58 am	
24 1st ♐ *Thanksgiving Day*	**25** 1st ♐ ☽ v/c 2:22 pm ☽ → ♑ 4:18 pm	**26** 1st ♑	
1	*2*	*3*	
8	*9*	*10*	

Aspects & Moon Phases

☌ Conjunction	0°	● New Moon	(1st Quarter)
✶ Sextile	60°	◐ Waxing Moon (2nd Quarter)	
☐ Square	90°	○ Full Moon	(3rd Quarter)
△ Trine	120°	◑ Waning Moon (4th Quarter)	
⚻ Quincunx	150°		
☍ Opposition	180°		

DECEMBER 2022

SU	M	T	W
27	28	29	30
4 2nd ♈ ☽ v/c 12:46 am ☽ → ♉ 6:38 am	**5** 2nd ♉	**6** 2nd ♉ ☽ v/c 2:02 pm ☽ → ♊ 3:49 pm ☿ → ♑ 5:08 pm	**○** 2nd ♊ Full Moon 11:08 pm *Long Nights Moon*
11 3rd ♋ ☽ v/c 1:49 pm ☽ → ♌ 3:09 pm	**12** 3rd ♌	**13** 3rd ♌ ☽ v/c 10:52 am	**14** 3rd ♌ ☽ → ♍ 3:45 am
18 4th ♎ ☽ v/c 5:35 pm ☽ → ♏ 10:31 pm	**19** 4th ♏	**20** 4th ♏ ♃ → ♈ 9:32 am ☽ v/c 9:45 pm	**21** 4th ♏ ☽ → ♐ 2:12 am ☉ → ♑ 4:48 pm *Yule* *Sun enters Capricorn* *Winter Solstice*
25 1st ♑ ☽ → ♒ 2:14 am *Christmas Day*	**26** 1st ♒ ☽ v/c 1:19 pm *Kwanzaa begins*	**27** 1st ♒ ☽ → ♓ 2:34 am	**28** 1st ♓
1	2	3	4

Eastern Standard Time (EST)

DECEMBER 2022

TH	F	SA	NOTES
2nd ♓ **1** ☽ v/c 9:44 pm ☽ → ♈ 11:41 pm	2nd ♈ **2**	2nd ♈ **3** Ψ D 7:15 pm	
3rd ♊ **8**	3rd ♊ **9** ☽ v/c 1:13 am ☽ → ♋ 2:49 am ♀ → ♑ 10:54 pm	3rd ♋ **10**	
3rd ♍ **15**	3rd ♍ **16** ◑ 4th Quarter 3:56 am ☽ v/c 2:13 pm ☽ → ♎ 2:49 pm	4th ♎ **17**	
4th ♐ **22** ☽ v/c 3:16 pm	4th ♐ **23** ● ☽ → ♑ 2:49 am New Moon 5:17 am *New Moon*	1st ♑ **24** ☽ v/c 10:11 pm *Christmas Eve*	
1st ♓ **29** ◐ ☽ v/c 1:21 am ☿ ℞ 4:32 am ☽ → ♈ 5:36 am 2nd Quarter 8:21 pm *Mercury retrograde*	2nd ♈ **30**	2nd ♈ **31** ☽ v/c 7:44 am ☽ → ♉ 12:08 pm *New Year's Eve*	
5	**6**	**7**	

ASPECTS & MOON PHASES

☌ Conjunction	0°	● New Moon	(1st Quarter)
✶ Sextile	60°	◐ Waxing Moon	(2nd Quarter)
☐ Square	90°	○ Full Moon	(3rd Quarter)
△ Trine	120°	◑ Waning Moon	(4th Quarter)
⚻ Quincunx	150°		
☍ Opposition	180°		